Contents

CHILD HEALTH NURSING BSC NURSING 3RD YEAR

PREVIOUS YEAR SOLVED QUESTIONS AND ANSWERS

RUTWIK UPENDRA BHALSHANKAR

CHAPTER ONE

Introduction and modern concept of child care

Short answer questions : -

Q 1. Role of a pediatric nurse

= Nurse is a person skilled or trained in caring for sick or injured people.

The role of the pediatric nurse is constantly changing. These changes are as a result of expanding medical and nursing practice, emerging challenges in different aspects of child care, consumer demands and technological advancements.

Primary Care Giver

- Provides preventive, promotive, curative and rehabilitative care in all levels of health services.
- Care of sick children , comfort , feeding , bathing , safety , etc
- At community set up, basic responsibilities include health assessment, immunization, primary health care and referral, etc.

Health Educator

- Delivers planned and incidental health teaching and information to the parents and significant others about prevention of illness, promotion or health maintenance.
- Creates awareness about healthy life styles and practices regarding child care.
- Characteristics of nurse teacher includes 4 Cs :
- C- Confidence
- C - Competence
- C - Communication
- C- Caring & empathy .

Counselor

- Provides - guidance to parents in health hazards of children .
- Helps - the parents and family members for independent decision making in different situations.
- Problem - solving approach.
- Active listener to establish a therapeutic relationship between parents and the child , making health care plans easier .

Social Worker

- Alleviate the social problems related to child health.
- Refers the child and family for social support .
- Participates in social services.

Team Coordinator

- Works along with other health team member.
- Coordinates the nursing care with other services for meeting the needs of child; e.g. , physician , social worker , surgeon , physiotherapist , dietician , etc.

- Maintain good interpersonal relationships with the child, family and health team members .

Manager

- Organize care , monitor and evaluate patient treatment for the successful outcome in the pediatric care units in hospitals , clinics and community .

Care Advocate

- The pediatric nurse acts as an advocate to safeguard the child's right , to assist and to provide best care from the health care team .
- Nurse acts as a representative for the child , family and other health care providers , e.g . , it can range from consulting dietary department for special foods to arrange team meeting to discuss plan of care with other health team members .

Researcher

- Research is an integral part of professional nursing.
- Participate in research projects related to child health.
- Provide the basis for the changes in the nursing practice and care of the children.
- Nurses are expected to be sensible enough in voicing out the needs of their patients.

Independent Practitioner

- It is an expanded role.
- Work in rural areas as nurse mid - wives and primary. care giver.
- Jointly practicing with the physician or independently .

Therapeutic Nurse

- Identifies the problem areas in their interaction with the family and child .
- Establishment of therapeutic relationship.

Recreationist

- The pediatric nurse plays supportive role for the child to provide play facilities for recreation and diversion .
- It helps to decrease crisis imposed by illness or hospitalization .

Community Health Nurse

- Monitors , anticipates , and responds to public health problems in population groups .
- Evaluates health risk factors of population groups . Participates in assessing and evaluating health care services.

Q 2. Qualities of a pediatric nurse.

= The good pediatric nurse must be:

1. Good observer
2. Honest and truthful
3. Sympathetic, kind, patient and cheerful
4. Love to work with children
5. Interested in family care
6. Able to provide teaching to children and their families
7. Friendly and diligent
8. Scientific knowledge, skill and expertise.

Q 3.Define paediatric nursing .

= The pediatrics is the branch of the medical science that deal with the care of children from conception to the adolescent in the health and illness ,

A Paediatric Nurse (also known as a Children's Nurse) is a nursing professional who cares for children and teens suffering from a variety of different conditions.

Q 4. Difference between adult and child care .

= DIFFERENCE BETWEEN ADULT AND CHILD

Children are not little adults. There are many differences between children, adolescents and adults - physiological, anatomical, cognitive, social, and emotional, which all impact on the way illness and disease present in children and young people, as well as the way healthcare is provided.

Anatomical and Physiological Differences

Larger BSA:

Children have a proportionately larger body surface area (BSA) than adults do. Smaller patient has greater ratio of surface area (skin) to size. As a result, children are at greater risk of excessive loss of

Thinner skin :

Children has thinner skin than adults . Their epidermis is thinner and under - keratinized , com pared with adults .

Rapidly dividing cells :

Children's cells divide more rapidly than adults to assist in their rapid rate of growth . As a result , children are more susceptible to the effects of radiation than adults .

Higher HR and RR :

Children have higher heart rates and respiratory rates than adults . In newborn , heart rate is 110-160 beats / min and respiratory rate is 35 40 breaths / min . Higher respiratory rates lead to pro portionately higher minute volumes . Hence , children have a greater risk of infection through pulmonary route . .

Immature blood brain - barrier :

Children have immature blood - brain barriers and enhanced central nervous system (CNS) receptivity . As a result , children may exhibit a prevalence of neurological symptoms

Higher metabolic rate :

More susceptible to contaminants in food or water and has greater risk for increased loss of water when ill or stressed .

Immature immune system :

Greater risk of infection , less hard immunity from some infection .

Mouth :

Infants tongue is large . Nasal and oral airway passages are relatively small making the baby more prone to airway obstruction . Nose breathers till 6 infections) . months of age (breathing difficulty in respiratory infections.)

Eyes:

No tears in early infancy due to poor functional development of lachrymal gland.

Eustachian tube: It is short and straight in children (10 ° in children and 40 ° in adults). Air sinuses are not fully developed. Sore throat extends to otitis media because of the closeness of it to throat.

Trachea:

Short and narrow trachea under 5 years. Hence they are susceptible to foreign body aspiration.

Glomerular filtration rate:

Concentration of urine in newborn is 800 mOsmol / L, whereas in adults it is 1400 mOsmol / L. GFR and tubular functions are lower in neonates than adults because of lower blood supply to kid ney, smaller pore size and less filtration power across nephron. GFR is 38 mL / min in neonate and 125 mL / min in adult.

Alimentary tract:

Water absorption is poor. Feces of the child are watery. Dehydration leads to circulatory failure within 24 hrs if treatment is inadequate.

Hepatic function:

Liver is immature in newborn. Pro duction of albumin, clotting factors and vitamin K are less. Iron reserve is less.

Central nervous system:

90% of brain growth takes place by 2 years of age. Nerve endings in the retina (rods and cones) are not fully developed. Thus, the images are blurred and colorless for a few weeks.

Q 5. FACTORS AFFECTING CHILD HEALTH

= Children are the most vulnerable population who face unusually high health risks as they grow. Major contributors to child health are:

1. **Maternal health**: Healthy mother with good nutritional status gives birth to a healthy baby. Child health may be impaired in case of inadequate nutrition or health problems during pregnancy.

2. **Low birth weight**: Children born with low birth weight often have an impaired immune function, which put them into higher risk of infection and death.

3. **Nutrition:** Children getting adequate quantity and qual ity of food grow healthy and are less prone to develop health problems. Malnutrition causes poor growth and more chances of infection. Inadequate breast feeding and poor complementary feeding may lead to malnu trition.

4. **Environment:** Environmental health factors contribute significantly to the incident of child mortality around the world. Inadequate sanitation, poor ventilation and housing condition, unsafe water supply and lack of ment of various health problems. good personal hygiene practices add to the develop

5. **Socioeconomic conditions:** Parental education, profession, income, housing, urban and rural living have great impact on health of children. Well economic condition of the family aids in good health facility and therefore children encounter less health problems.

6. **Health policy of government:** Sound health policy of the government helps in reducing health problems in children.

Q 6. Rights of children's

= The child is defined as a person in 0 – 18 years of the age group .

The general assembly affirmed that the decleration of the rights of the child aims to ensure that the he may have a happy child hood and enjoy . the right and freedom for his own good and for good society .

Following are the Some rights of the child :

Special rights for the child as per commissions recommendations are :

Right to safe environment .

Right to food

Right to health care .

Right to education

Right to freedom

Right against child marriage .

Right to be free from any discrimination

Right to be protection from any abuse .

Right to be heard and participate freely .

Right to family life .

Right to leisure and free time .

Q 7. Child welfare policy and explain about any one .

= **NATIONAL CHILD WELFARE POLICY**

Keeping in view the problems and challenges faced by the Indian children, laws have been introduced and various policies and programs are being implemented for the welfare of children in India.

Child Welfare Policy

1. UN Convention on the Rights of the Child, 11th Dec, 1992.
2. HMBU The National Policy for Children, Aug 22, 1974

3. National Policy on Education, 1986
4. The National Policy on Child Labor, August, 1987
5. National Nutrition Policy, 1993
6. National Plan for SAARC decade for the Girl Child 1990 – 2000
7. UN Millennium Summit - MDG (Sep 30, 2000)
8. National Health Policy, 2002 National Charter for Children, 2003
9. National Plan of Action for Children, 2005
10. The Commissions for Protection of the Child Rights Act, 2005
11. The National Policy for Children, 2013

The National Policy for Children, 1974

The National Policy for Children, 1974 was adopted on 22nd August 1974 in order to address the emerging challenges relating to child rights. The nation's children are a supremely important asset. Their nurture and solicitude are our responsibility.

The following policy measures were taken up by the government :

- Services before and after birth
- Comprehensive health services.
- Nutrition services with the objective of removing deficiencies in the diet of children.
- Free and compulsory education for all children up to the age of 14.
- Informal education to drop outs.
- Promotion of physical education, games, sports and other types of recreational, as well as cultural and scientific activities in schools and community centers.
- Protection against the neglect , cruelty and exploitation .
- Equal opportunity to weaker sections , physically challenged and delinquents children

The National Policy on Child Labor (August, 1987)

The National Policy on Child Labour declared in August, 1987, contains strategies for tackling the problems of child labour.

It includes:

- Child Labour (Prohibition & Regulation) Act, 1986 to prohibit the engagement of children in certain employ ments and to regulate the conditions of work of chi dren in certain other employments.
- General development programs for benefiting children wherever possible.
- Launching of projects for the welfare of working children in areas of high concentration of child labor.
- Rehabilitation of child labour.

The special schools / rehabilitation centres provide:

- Non - formal / bridge education Skilled / vocational training
- Mid day meal
- Stipend @ Rs.150 / - per child per month

Health care facilities through a doctor appointed for a group of 20 schools.

National Nutrition Policy, 1993

- It provides the following strategies:
- Nutrition intervention for specially vulnerable population .
- Fortification of essential foods.
- Popularization of low cost nutritious food.
- Control of the micronutrient deficiencies amongst vulnerable groups .
- Various nutritional programmes
- Nutritional surveillance .

Q 8 Child welfare agencies and explain about any one .

= There are many national and international organizations working for the welfare of the most vulnerable population of our country. Following are a few of them.

Indian Council for Child Welfare

It was established in 1952 to secure the rights and protec tion of Indian children. Their activities are:

- Advocating children's rights
- Creches for children of working and ailing mothers .
- Training programs for child care workers Sponsorship for school education of under - privileged children M L Iron / Hb status.
- Programs for children in difficult circumstances.
- Programs with special focus on the girl child education centers and support services .
- Honoring children for bravery.
- Honoring child artists .
- Projects for street and working children .
- Scrutiny of adoption cases .
- Rehabilitation of abandoned children .
- Institutional and day care services for differently abled children .

CHILDLINE India Foundation

CHILDLINE India Foundation (CIF) is the nodal agency of the Union Ministry of Women and Child Development acting as the parent organization for setting up, managing and monitoring the CHILDLINE 1098 service all over the country. CHILDLINE 1098 service is a 24 - hr free emer gency phone outreach service for children in need of care and protection.

UNICEF

UNICEF has been working in India since 1949. This is the largest international organization in the country working exclusively for children. UNICEF is fully committed to working with the Government of India to ensure that every child born in this vast and complex country gets the best start in life, thrives and develops to his or her full poten tial.

They work in the field of health, education, nutrition, environmental hygiene, HIV, protection, and emergency.

Goals are:

- To ensure the necessary reduction in maternal, infant, and young child mortality.
- To reduce and prevent malnutrition and to improve the development of children under 3 years of age, especially those in marginalized groups.
- To introduce range of replicable models for sanitation, hygiene, and water supply.
- To build a protective environment in which children can live and develop in the full respect of their funda mental rights.

There are many other child welfare agencies such as Save the Children Fund, Child in Need Institute, CARE, WHO, UNESCO, USAID, FAO, etc.

Q 9. Impact of hospitalisation on child .

= Illness and hospitalisation are stress full experiences for child and families . Long term illness and hospitalisation has a potential to negatively impact child motor , cognitive, emotional and social development.

Impact of hospitalisation on child's : illness and hospitalisation has a potential to negatively . Each child perceives illness and hospitalisation uniquely . Common stressors in child are includes

Separation anxiety , loss of control , Bodily Injury and Pain .

1 Infant :

Separation anxiety : The infant passes through the three phases of Separation anxiety. In initial phase , infants demonstrate protest by crying and rejecting attention of other care giver .

Then the infant moves to the next phase of despair, he becomes quite and withdrawn, refuses food, appears sad, listless, and lonely. If the separation continues the infant enters the final phase of separation anxiety known as detachment, showing interests in surrounding, forming new relations, reluctance to meet parents, etc. In this phase the infant is actually showing the sign of resignation.

Loss of Control

According to Erikson, infant develops trust or mistrust during care given by parents or significant others. Infant develops reduced sense of control due to preference given to the hospital routines, their treatment needs and neglect to their emotional needs.

2. Toddlers :

Separation anxiety - Separation anxiety causes greatest stress to hospitalized toddler and preschooler. During the pro test phase, the toddler asks for parents all the time, showsTemper tantrum on parents departure or return, refuses to maintain routines of mealtime, bedtime or toileting.

During the second phase toddler withdraws self, engages in thumb sucking, bedwetting although previously toilet trained, develops sleep disturbances. Toddler does not protest any painful procedure. In the final phase, the toddler does not react to parents' visit or departure, accepts all hospital routines and during discharge may turn away from parents and become suspicious.

Loss of Control : Sense of autonomy, which develops during toddlerhood is disturbed or threatened due to hospitalization. Hindrance to normal daily activities, forceful confinement in bed may cause negativism in terms of temper tantrum. It exhibits as regression like refusing food other than usual food at home, demanding bottle, etc. This regression to earlier behaviour in search of security and comfort, may be threatening ening for future development.

Loss of Bodily Injury and Pain : Fear of unknown, discomfort with restraints and anticipated fear of bodily injury or pain cause toddler resisting for physical examination, diagnostic or therapeutic procedures. They react more than infants if they are separated from parents, restrained, watching parental apprehension or having previous traumatic experience.

3. Preschoolers

Separation Anxiety

Preschoolers can tolerate brief periods of separation from parents as they are more secure interpersonally than toddlers. They express protest by crying quietly and sometimes refusing food, medication, constantly asking when the parents will come to visit. They exhibit anger by breaking toys, hitting others, etc. Some children can regress in behaviour and become overly dependent on their parents.

Loss of Control

Preschoolers expect to maintain their independence during hospitalization. They experience loss of control by mobility restriction, change of daily routine, and enforced dependency. They view everything on their own egocentric perspective. Hence, they perceive hospitalization as the punishment for real or imagined misdeeds, which develops a sense of shame or guilt in them.

Loss of Bodily Injury and Pain :

The loss interest in other activities and centre of attention on affected part of the body . preschooler are sensitive about the bodily changes caused by the diseases and its treatment .

4. School Age Children

Separation Anxiety

School age children have better understanding and coping ability. Young school age children need parental security and undergo phases of separation anxiety as they have just started going to school and still struggling to cope with that separation. This can be demonstrated as enuresis, night terrors, insomnia or nail biting, etc. Older school age children feel more separated from peers and detached from daily activities in school. Feeling boredom, isolation, exam tension are common in school aged hospitalized child.

Loss of Control

According to Erikson's stage of industry vs inferiority, school age children feel helpless, dependent on others due to physical limitation. Dependence in the form of enforced bed rest, use of bed pan, food of hospital choice, lack of privacy, strict bed time routine, moving in stretcher or wheelchair etc causes inferiority among them. They also fear losing friends during the course of hospitalization.

Loss of Bodily Injury and Pain

The hospitalized school age child is apprehensive about bodily injury and pain. But they are relaxed during physical examination as their understanding about body parts and functions are better than younger children. They express less overt behavior like crying or motor aggression. They fear death and mutilation as they understand cause and effect of illness.

5.Adolescence :

Separation Anxiety

Response to hospitalization is varied in case of adoles cents. Some may feel confused whether to seek parental presence or some others may enjoy freedom or period of independence. Loss of peer group contact may cause frustration among them .

Loss of Control

Hospital rule constaints to there independence and leads to frustration . the demands of treatment interfers with the normal activities of the adolescents , Further interfering with social development and consequently this may result in depression and feeling of hopelessness. They may react with the rejection, uncooperativeness or withdrawal .

Q 10 . Pre and post operative care of the child .

= General Aspects of Pre - and Postoperative Pediatric Care Preoperative Care The nursing activities in preoperative period include assessment, identification of health problems, preoperative health teaching, and preparation of the child.

Psychological Preparation

- Reduce fear of separation, physical harm, pain or death by giving simple concise and age appropriate informa tion to the child and family.
- Explain the procedure and postoperative equipments in a play full way to prevent fear of unknown.
- Clarify doubts and queries of parents and child.

Physical Preparation

- Physical preparation is necessary for preventing perioperative complications.
- Except in emergency situation children should prefer ably be free of respiratory complications and signs of malnutrition.
- Children must have nothing by mouth before surgery for the prescribed period according to the age.
- Good hydration is needed before NPO.
- Bathe the child and give mouth care in the morning.
- The incision over or the part involved in surgery must be washed and inspected. Shaving may be needed.
- Mouth should be checked for loose teeth particularly in children. If present it should be reported to the anesthetist to prevent aspiration.
- Remove clips or pins from hair.
- The child should be given warm and loose hospital gown.
- Allow eye glasses or hearing aid to the operation theatre and keep them in recovery room for postoperative use.
- Check identification band to see whether it is legible and secure.
- Premedication like sedatives and analgesics are usually given 2 hrs before surgery, except in emergency situation.
- The nurse should chart whether the child has passed urine and had a bowel movement. Enemas are not given regularly, except in certain conditions.
- Nostrils should be cleansed carefully before surgery especially in newborns and infants (hard crusts may be softened with a solution of sodium bicarbonate, Normal saline or even warm

water) as crusts may obstruct the airway.
- Ensure that consent form is signed by parents; All laboratory test reports are included in the chart.
- The child may take favorite toy with him to operatheater and may be allowed to keep until he is under anesthesia.
- Parents should be allowed to accompany the child to the operation site if they desire.
- Parents should be informed where to wait till the surge is over and whether the child will be shifted to recovery room after surgery or to his unit directly.

Postoperative Care

- Nursing activities in the postoperative phase include monitoring of the child for response to surgery, preventing complication, promoting early recovery, health teaching for post operative exercises and care at home after discharge.
- Immediate Postoperative Care
- Receive the child in recovery room with detail information..
- Position appropriately to maintain patent airway and prevent aspiration preferably on his side or abdomen.
- Monitor vital signs every 15 min. Observe conditions and placement of dressing.
- Check and mark any apparent drainage from operated site.
- Monitor IV fluid for accurate rate of infusion and possible infiltration.

Care after Recovery

- The child should be carefully handled and protected from injury.
- The urinary catheter should be connected to drainage bag and stabilized properly to bed.
- Check the activity level, general condition, and adequacy of ventilation.
- Adequate pain management according to child’s need.

- Observe time of voiding and monitor intake and put out.
- Reunite parents and child to reduce anxiety. Oral fluids may be started after the following criteria are observed: (a) color of the aspirate is clear, (b) peri staltic movements are heard, (c) flatus are passed. Oral fluid should be started while the infusion is still going on. If well tolerated, infusion is gradually discontinued. Diet can be started from clear liquid, full liquid, soft and then regular diet.
- Change position frequently.
- Progressive ambulation is advised to restore gas trointestinal function and prevent complications of pneumonia, thrombosis and pressure ulcer.

Observe for Postoperative Complication

- Observe patient's skin color and temperature changes.
- Watch for signs of shock such as low blood pressure, rapid pulse, cold moist pale or cyanotic skin, dilated S pupils, and restlessness.
- Observe for other signs such as hemorrhage from wound, vomiting, hypoxia, abdominal distension, hypostatic pneumonia, retention of urine, wound infection, or thrombophlebitis.
- Notify physician if any of the above signs are present.

Health Teaching

- Demonstrate postoperative exercises and encourage performing.
- Educate dietary requirement for the child.
- Teach home care of the child depending on the surgi cal procedure.

Q 11. ICDS Scheme

INTRODUCTION

Integrated Child Development Services is a government program in India which provides nutritional meals, preschool education, primary healthcare, immunization, health check-up and referral services to children under 6 years of age and their mothers.

ICDS Scheme represents one of the world's largest and most unique programmes for early childhood development. ICDS is the foremost symbol of India's commitment to her children. The main beneficiaries of the programme were aimed to be the girl child up to her adolescence, all children below 6 years of age, pregnant and lactating mothers.

Purpose of initiation

- Routine MCH services not reaching target population.
- Nutritional component not covered by health services.
- Need for community participation.

OBJECTIVES

- To improve the nutritional status of preschool children 0-6 years of age group.
- To lay the foundation of proper psychological development of the child
- To reduce the incidence of mortality, morbidity malnutrition and school drop out
- To achieve effective coordination of policy and implementation in various departments to promote child development
- To enhance the capability of the mother to look after the normal health and nutritional needs of of the child through proper nutrition and health education

PACKAGE OF SERVICES

- Beneficiaries Services Pregnant women Health check up, immunization, supplementary nutrition, health and nutrition education.
- Nursing mothers Health check up, supplementary nutrition, health and nutrition education Other women 15 – 45 years Nutrition and health education
- Children less than 3 yrs Health check up, immunization, supplementary nutrition, referral services
- Children in age 3 -6 yrs Health check up, immunization, supplementary nutrition, referral services, non formal education
- Adolescent girls 11 – 18 yrs. Supplementary nutrition and health education

COMPONENT OF ICDS

- Health Check-ups.
- Immunization.
- Growth Promotion and Supplementary Feeding.
- Referral Services.
- Early Childhood Care and Pre-school Education.
- Nutrition and Health Education.

SUPPLEMENTARY NUTRITION

- Supplementary nutrition is given to children below 6 years, and nursing and expectant mothers from low income group. The aim is to supplement nutritional intake as follows:
- Each child up to 6 years of age to get 300 calories and 8-10 grams of protein
- Each adolescent girl to get 500 calories and 20-25grams of protein
- Each pregnant women and lactating mother to get 500 calories and 20-25 gms of protein
- Each malnourished child to get 600 calories and 16-20 grams of protein

IMMUNIZATION-

Immunization of children against 6 vaccine preventable disease is being done, while for expectant mothers, immunization against tetanus is recommended.

HEALTH CHECK UP

- Record of weight and height of children at periodical intervals
- Watch over milestones
- Immunization
- Deworming
- General check up for detection of disease
- Treatment of diseases like diarrhea, ARI
- Prophylaxis against vitamin A deficiency and anemia
- Referral of serious cases
- Antenatal care of expectant mothers
- Post natal care of nursing mothers and care of new born infants

Non-formal Pre-School Education (PSE)

Children between the ages 3-6 years are imparted non- formal pre-school education in an angandwadi in each village with about 1000 population. The objective is to provide opportunities to develop desirable attitude, values and behaviour pattern among children. Locally produced inexpensive toys and material are used in organizing play and creative activity.

Referral Services:

- During health check-ups and growth monitoring, sick or malnourished children, in need of prompt medical attention, are referred to the Primary Health Centre or its sub-centre.
- Nutrition and Health Education: Health education is given to womens so that they can look after their own health, nutrition and development needs as well as that of their children and families.

THE ICDS TEAM:

- The ICDS team comprises the Anganwadi Workers, Anganwadi Helpers, Supervisors, Child Development Project Officers (CDPOs) and District Programme Officers (DPOs).
- Medical officers, Auxiliary Nurse Midwife (ANM) and Accredited Social Health Activist (ASHA) form a team with the ICDS functionaries to achieve convergence of different services.

Q 12 Concept of modern pediatrics nursing

= The health of children has historically been of vital importance to all societies because children are the basic resources of the future of mankind. In any country, mothers and children constitute approximately 60% of the population.

DEFINITION AND CONCEPT OF PEDIATRICS

The word "pediatric" is derived from Greek word 'pedia' meaning child and 'iatri' means treatment and 'ics' meaning branch of science. Thus, pediatrics is defined as the branch of medical science that deals with child development and care and with the diseases of childhood and their treatment.

Pediatrics refers to the comprehensive and continued care of children. It serves both in wellness and illness.

MODERN PEDIATRICS

It is difficult to say, when Pediatrics became a separate specialty. It developed gradually as the knowledge of developmental needs of children increased in society. Pediatrics as a specialty developed with the establishment of Department of Pediatrics in various medical colleges, establishment of separate pediatric units for children in general hospitals and fondling homes. Today we no longer consider children as miniature adults. Childhood is considered a separate phase of life.

The present concept of health care of child focuses on prevention of illness and promotion of health rather than treatment of illnesses alone.

Present focus of pediatrics is shifting from traditional to process oriented one that is based on sound scientific rationale.

Focus of pediatrics is shifting:

Shift From Focus On:

Shift From	Focus On
1. Disease centered care.	Child centered care within the family system.
2. Discouraging the families on neglect of female child.	Taking special care of female child as she is future mother.
3. Starting care for woman after she became pregnant.	Health education on planned parenthood and guarding maternal health before conception.
4. Special care of the sick child in hospital.	Comprehensive care of the child from the day of conception throughout the developmental years of childhood.
5. Caring for the physical condition of the child in isolation (hospital).	Holistic care of the child that is family centered.
6. Illness oriented care.	Health promotion oriented care.
7. Not allowing parents to be with the child in hospital and having rigid visiting hours.	Ensuring that child must have one parent with him/her in the hospital and having flexible visiting hours.
8. Care was only hygiene and treatment oriented.	Warmth and love oriented.
9. Providing routine care.	Quality care in terms of play, recreation, nutrition, etc.
10. Traditional practices.	Evidence based practice.

CHAPTER TWO

Growth and Development.

Q 1 . Define growth and development .

= 1. Growth : Growth refers to an increase in size or mass of the tissues . It is largely attributed to multiplication of cells and increase in intracellular substance . It can be measured in inches centimeters , kilograms and pounds . So it is a quantitative term .

2. Development : Development specifies maturation of functions or physiological maturation The term ' development ' is used to refer progressive increase in skills and capacity to function . It is a qualitative change in child's functioning and is difficult to measure . Development is the result of maturation and learning .

Q 2. Principals of growth and development .

= 1. Growth : Growth refers to an increase in size or mass of the tissues . It is largely attributed to multiplication of cells and increase in intracellular substance . It can be measured in inches centimeters , kilograms and pounds . So it is a quantitative term .

2. Development : Development specifies maturation of functions or physiological maturation The term ' development ' is used to refer progressive increase in skills and capacity to function . It is a qualitative change in child's functioning and is difficult to measure . Development is the result of maturation and learning .

Principles / Characteristics of Growth and Development.

Gessel (founder of clinical child psychology) has concluded from genetic studies of children - "although no two children are alike, all normal children tend to follow a general sequence of growth". There are certain basic predictable characteristics or principles of growth and development which are as follows:

1. Development is Similar for all: All children follow similar pattern of development with one stage leading into the next. Every child passes through similar stages. For example, baby learns to stand before he walks, similarly, baby draws circle before a square.

2. Development Proceeds from General to Specific: In motor as well as mental responses, general activity always precedes specific activity. Before birth, fetus moves the whole body but is incapable of making specific movements. Generalized body movements occur before fine motor control is achieved. For example, first the infant moves whole body in the womb and later starts moving his hands. Similarly infants move hands first and then learn using fingers.

3.Development is Continuous: Development is a continuous process, starting from conception and ending at death. It is continuous but sometimes rapid and at times slow. For example, speech in a child does not develop overnight, the child coos, gurgles and makes sounds first and then slowly and gradually learns words and then language develops.

4. Development proceeds at Different Rates: Growth and development is a continuous process which is rapid at times and at times slows down. Rapid growth occurs during fetal life and infancy and it slows down during school age. A growth spurt occurs in puberty and early adolescence but it slows down during adulthood and old age.

5. There is Correlation in Growth and Development: Correlation in physical and mental abilities is especially marked. There is a marked relationship between sexual maturation and patterns of interest and behavior.

6. Development comes from Maturation and Learning: Sudden appearance of certain traits that develop through maturation is quite common. For example, a baby may start walking overnight.

Behavioral changes occur at the time of puberty suddenly without any reason. Learning comes from exercise and efforts on the part of an individual. Unless the child had opportunity for learning, many of his hereditary potentials will never reach their optimum development. For example, a child may have aptitude for music because of his superior neuromuscular organization, but if he is deprived of opportunities for practice and systematic training, he will not reach his maximum potential. Intrinsic growth is a gift of nature. Innate capacities should be stimulated by positive environmental factors.

7. There are Individual Differences: Although pattern of development is similar for all children, each child follows a predictable pattern in his own way and at his own rate. Each child with his unique heredity and nature (environment) will progress at its own rate in terms of size, shape, capacity and developmental status.

8. Early Development is More Significant than Later Development: If the foundation of a building is strong, the building will be strong. Similarly, favorable conditions during infancy lead to growth of child into a healthy adult. If the conditions during prenatal period and postnatal period are unfavorable, there is a damaging effect on later growth and development of the child.

9. Development Proceeds in Stages: Development is not abrupt, it proceeds in stages that are as follows:.

- Prenatal period: From conception to birth
- Neonatal Period: Birth to four weeks Infancy: Four weeks to 1 year
- Toddler: From 1-3 years Pre school: 3-6 years (early childhood)
- School age: 6-12 years (late childhood)
- Adolescence: From puberty to beginning of adulthood (13-18 years)

10. There are predictable patterns of growth and development: Both during prenatal and postnatal period, growth and development follow two patterns.

- Cephalocaudal
- Proximodistal

According to cephalocaudal pattern, development spreads over the body from head to foot. This means that improvement in structure and functions of the body comes first in the head region, than in trunk and lastly the legs. According to proximodistal pattern, development proceeds from near to far, i.e. from the central axis of the body towards the periphery or extremities. During the prenatal period, the head and trunk develop fully and then the limb buds appear. Slowly the arms lengthen, followed by forearms and lastly the fingers. Functionally also, the baby starts using his arms before his hands and fingers.

Q 3. Factors Affecting the growth and development

•

= 1. Growth : Growth refers to an increase in size or mass of the tissues . It is largely attributed to multiplication of cells and increase in intracellular substance . It can be measured in inches centimeters , kilograms and pounds . So it is a quantitative term .

2. Development : Development specifies maturation of functions or physiological maturation The term ‘ development ’ is used to refer progressive increase in skills and capacity to function . It is a qualitative change in child’s functioning and is difficult to measure . Development is the result of maturation and learning .

Factors Affecting Growth and Development

Growth and development depends not only on one but a combination of many factors. The typical pattern of growth and development is regulated by a complex balance between heredity or genetic constitutionand environmental factors. Heredity determine the extent to which growth and development is possible and environment determines the degree to which the maximum potential is achieved.

1. **Heredity / Genetic Factors**

i . Heredity : It refers to the genetic constitution of an individual which is established during conception . It is that property by which offsprings have nature and characteristics of parents or ancestors . From parents , the child receives a combination of parental genes . Every individual's supply of genes is given to him at the time of conception . Color of eyes , hair , facial features , structure of body , physical peculiarities , blood group , etc. are determined entirely by heredity . It is because of heredity that members of a family have physical resemblance to each other .

ii . Race : Growth potential of children of different racial groups is different .

iii . Sex : Sex of the baby is determined at conception . After birth , male infant is long and heavier than female infant . At the age of 1 year , there is no difference in the length and weight of male and female infants . During puberty , growth spurt occurs and boys become taller and heavier than girls of their age .

iv . Biorhythm and Maturation : Daughters often reach menarche at same age as their mothers had . Also the length of menstrual cycle is same as that of mother .

V. Genetic Disorders : Growth and development are adversely affected by certain genetic disorders .

These disorders are of two types :

a . Chromosomal abnormalities like Turner's syndrome and Down's syndrome which cause growth retardation

b . Gene mutations may lead to metabolic defects like galactosemia .

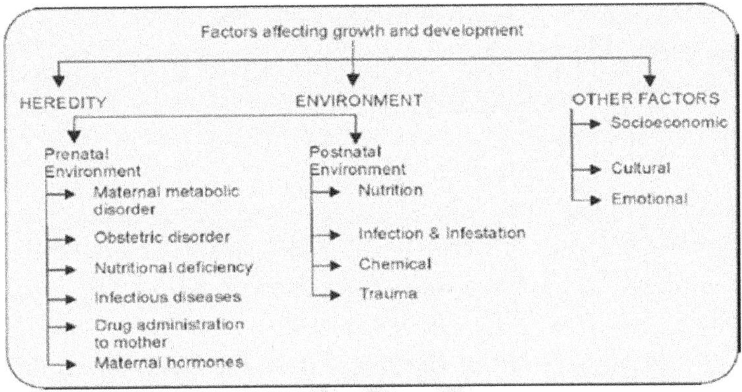

II . Environmental Factors Although each human being at birth has a genetically determined physical , mental and biochemical potential , but this potential may or may not be reached because of environmental Influences . Stimulation for development of innate abilities comes from the environment which may be favorable or unfavorable .

a . Prenatal Environment : The environment which the fetus gets in utero , before birth is known as prenatal environment . This environment provides nutrition and does gas exchange also . The uterus protects fetus from adverse effects of external conditions . A substandard or diseased Intrauterine environment has an adverse effect on growing fetus . For example , intrauterine rubella infection produces severe reduction in quantity of cells in many organs while toxemia in late pregnancy leads to significant increase in cell size though the number of cells is normal . The factors affecting fetal growth are as follows :

i . Nutritional deficiency in mother : Maternal under nutrition and anemia leads to intrauterine growth retardation and consequently small size of fetus .

iii . Obstetric Disorders : Obstetric disorders like pregnancy induced hypertension , pre eclampsia , multiple pregnancy , malposition of fetus produces fetal growth restriction .

iii. Metabolic Disorders in Mother : Disorders of metabolism like Diabetes mellitus leads to large size of fetus .

iv . Infections : Maternal rubella infection occurring during first trimester of pregnancy results in congenital malformation in fetus . Children with birth defects cannot grow at an optimal rate . Other maternal infections like Syphilis , Hepatitis B , HIV , Cytomegalovirus inclusion , Toxoplasmosis , etc. may be transmitted to the fetus which may arrest or retard the growth of fetus .

V. Administration of Certain Drugs : Consumption of certain drugs like Thalidomide by mother during first trimester of pregnancy adversely affects embryo and leads to birth defects . These drugs are called teratogenic agents .

vi. Influence of Maternal Hormones :

Thyroxine : Human fetus secretes thyroxine from 12th week of gestation . Thyroxine deficiency in mother retards skeletal maturation in fetus . Maternal myxedema results in hypothyroidism in fetus .

Insulin : Insulin stimulates fetal growth . In mothers with diabetes , fetus is usually large with excessive birth weight . As matemal blood sugar level is high , fetal blood sugar is also elevated . This leads to hyperplasia of islet cells of fetal pancreas leading to excessive insulin secretion resulting in macrosomia .

b .Postnatal Environment : The environment that the baby gets after birth is known as postnatal environment . This environment determines the pace and pattern of growth and development . Postnatal environmental factors affecting growth and development are :

1. **Nutrition :** Growth of children suffering from protein - energy malnutrition , Anemia and Vitamin deficiency diseases (like rickets) is severely affected . Also overeating and over nutrition leads to obesity .

2. . **Infections and Infestations** : Persistent or recurrent diarrhea and respiratory tract infections are common causes of growth impairment . Systemic infections and parasitic infestations usually decrease the velocity of growth
3. . **Chemical Agents** : Consumption of androgenic hormones accelerates skeletal growth .
4. . **Trauma** : Fracture of end of bone , damages the growing epiphysis and thus hampers skeletal growth . Head injury may cause brain damage and seriously jeopardize mental development of the child .

III . Other Factors

i . Socioeconomic Condition : The environment of children born in lower socioeconomic groups is usually less favorable than those in middle and upper groups . The parents with poor financial condition usually cannot take proper care of their children , as they do not have money to buy essentials of health and diet . Poverty , crowded and unhygienic living conditions lead to retardation of growth and development in children .

ii . Cultural Influences : Culture influences the child rearing and infant feeding practices in community . There are many cultural taboos against consumption of particular food stuffs . This affects the nutritional status and growth of the children . For example , some communities are strictly vegetarian and do not consume egg , meat , etc. The children of these communities do not get proteins of high biologic value due to which their growth may be retarded . Similarly in some communities , colostrum is not fed to the child as it is considered impure yellow milk . This practice devoids the children of many nutritional substances and antibodies present in colostrum which makes these children susceptible to infections thereby affecting growth .

iii . Emotional Factors : Children from broken homes and orphanages do not grow and develop at an optimal rate . Anxiety , insecurity , lack of emotional support and love from the family affects the neurochemical regulation of hormones which affect growth and development of children On the other hand , parents who had happy childhood and have cheerful personality transmit these characters to their children.

Q 4. Aspects of growth and development .

= Growth and development have following aspects :

Growth

Growth

Biological growth Sensory Growth Motar Growth

Developmental :

Intellectual Moral Emotional Sexual Social Language.

1. Growth : Growth refers to an increase in size or mass of the tissues . It is largely attributed to multiplication of cells and increase in intracellular substance . It can be measured in inches centimeters , kilograms and pounds . So it is a quantitative term .

2. Development : Development specifies maturation of functions or physiological maturation The term ' development ' is used to refer progressive increase in skills and capacity to function . It is a qualitative change in child's functioning and is difficult to measure . Development is the result of maturation and learning .

A. Growth

a . Biologic Growth : Changes in body result from growth of different parts of body . The National center for Health Statistics (NCHS) made a massive survey of characteristics of growth - length or height , weight and head circumference . These are the parameters for assessing growth in children .

i . Length or Height : Length or height increases from birth to maturity . Rapid increase in height occurs during infancy and adolescence . The average length of a newborn is 45-50 cm and it increases at the rate of 2-2.5 cm / month for first six months and then 1.25 cm / month during next six months . At the age of 1 year length is 75 cm . The height of infant doubles at the age of 4 years and triples at 13 years .

ii . Weight : Weight is the best gross index of health and nutritional status of children . The average weight of a newborn is 2.5-3.5 kg . There is initially loss of weight during first 10 days of life due to adjustment to extrauterine life , inadequate feeds and digestive adaptation . After 10 days of life , baby gains about 30 gms weight per day for 5-6 months so weight doubles at 6 months of age and becomes about 5-6 kg . Thereafter weight gain becomes grams per day during next 6 months . So at the age of one year weight becomes triple of birth weight (about 7.5-8 kg) . At the age of 2 % years weight becomes four times the birth weight that is 10-12 kg .

iii . Head Circumference : The head circumference is an important measurement since it is related to intracranial volume . An increase in head circumference indicates rate of brain growth . At birth , the normal head circumference is 33 cm approximately and it increases at the rate of about ½ inch per month during first 6 months and then at the rate of ¼ inch per month during next 6 months . The head circumference is 40 cm at 3 months and 45 cm at 1 year of age .

iv . Chest Circumference : The chest is barrel shaped at birth and the anterioposterior and transverse diameters are equal . Gradually the transverse diameter increases , causing width to become greater than the anterioposterior diameter . At birth chest circumference is 31cm and at the end of 1year head circumference becomes equal to chest circumference , thereafter only chest circumference increases .

b . Motor Growth : Motor development depends on maturation of muscular , skeletal and nervous system . The motor development follows cephalocaudal and proximodistal pattern . Motor development is of two types.

i. Gross Motor

Gross Motor development leads to acquisition of increasing mobility and independent movements . Gross motor activities include turning , sitting , standing and walking .

ii . Fine Motor

Fine Motor development leads to acquisition of motor dexterity like use of hand and fingers , palmar grasp and release , pincer grasp etc.

c . Sensory Growth : Although sensory system is functional at birth , the child gradually learns the process of associating meaning with a perceived stimulus . Most active senses at birth are sense of taste and smell . As myelinization of nervous system occurs , the child is able to respond to specific stimuli . The visual system is last to mature , at about 6-7 years of age .

B. Development

Many theories have been devised to study development of different aspects in children .

1. Intellectual Development theory by Jean Piaget
2. Moral Development theory by Jean Plaget and Kohlberg
3. Psychosocial Development theory by Eric H Erikson
4. Spiritual Development theory by James W Fowler
5. Sexual Development theory by Sigmund Freud
6. Emotional Development theory by Eric H .

Q 5. Discuss the Psychosocial Development theory.

= Psychosocial Development The theory of Erikson Concerning ' Psychosocial Development ' states that emotional or personality development is a continuous process which has the following stages

i . Trust Versus Mistrust (Birth to one year - Infant) : Infants learn to trust the adults , are sensitive to their needs . A negative usually the parents who care for them outcome of the period of infancy is the sense of mistrust which develops if the basic needs of infant are not met .

ii . Autonomy Versus Shame (One to three years - Toddler) : Infants develop from clinging , dependent creatures into individuals with mind and will of their own . The three major psychosocial tasks of toddlerhood are gaining self - control , developing autonomy and increasing independence . If the child succeeds in development of autonomy he develops feeling of self - esteem , but if he does not succeed , he doubts his abilities and develops a sense of shyness and shame .

iii. Initiative Versus guilt (Three to six years - Preschool child) : This is a period of very energetic play and active imagination . The child can develop a sense of accomplishment and satisfaction in his or her activities . As the child oversteps his or her limits he or she experiences a feeling of guilt .

iv . Industry Versus Inferiority (Six to twelve years- School age child) : Children in this age have a strong sense of duty . Their energy is channeled into activities such as school projects , sports and hobbies . These concrete endeavors become the child's work and industry , feeling of inferiority may develop . bring a sense of accomplishment . If the children are not able to achieve a sense of

V. Identity Versus Role Diffusion (Twelve to fifteen years - Beginning of Adolescence) : Two major tasks for adolescents are figuring out who they are and what is their place in the world . Success in this period makes the individual well adjusted , stable and mature . Individuals who have not experienced any active exploration nor made a commitment to any occupation , develop identity diffusion .

vi . Intimacy versus self - absorption (Late Adolescence) : In this stage the adolescents focus on forming intimate relationships with others . They develop a sense of intimacy with peers . Failure to establish such intimacy results in psychological isolation , i.e. keeping relations without warmth .

Q 6. Discuss the Psychosexual Developmental theory.

= Psychosexual Development

In accordance with the view that basic human motivation is sexual drive , Sigmund Freud developed a psychosexual theory of human development from infancy onwards , divided into series of psychosexual stages . Freud named these stages as **Oral , Anal , Phallic , Latency and Genital** . Each stage focuses on gratification of libido through a particular erogenous zone of the body . If a child does not successfully complete a stage , he or she would develop a fixation that would later influence adult personality and behavior .

- **Oral stage (Infancy , the first year of life) :** This is the first stage exemplified by infant's pleasure in nursing . Gratification of needs center around feeding .
- **Anal stage : (Toddler Period , 2-3 years) :** This stage revolves around interest in body functions and gratification of needs is by retaining and expelling faces .
- **Phallic Stage (Preschool period , end of 3rd year of age up to 5 years) :** In this stage the site of greatest sensual pleasure is genital region . In this stage oedipal conflict arises , wherein a boy desires for his mother but has a fear of castration by rival father . In this stage the boys fixate on the mother as a sexual object (known as Oedipus Complex) but the child eventually overcomes and represses this desire because of its taboo nature . Freud attempts to formulate a comparable process for girls fixating on fathers (known as Electra Complex) . During this stage the child loves parents of opposite sex and takes them as provider of sensual satisfaction .
- **Latency stage (School age , 6-12 years) :** This is repressive or dormant stage of psychosexual development .

Genital Stage (About 12 years to adulthood) : During this stage , developing human matures from pleasure seeking infant into sexually mature adult who is free to enter heterosexual relationships .

Q 7. Breast feeding advantages.

= breast feeding is the wholesome food for the baby . breast feeding is the most effective way to provide baby with a caring environment and complete nutrition . it meets the nutritional as well as emotional needs of the baby . UNICEF and WHO recommended exclusive breast feeding to babies until six month of age.

Advantages of Breast Feeding

Breast feeding is ideal for the neonates . It has several advantages both for the baby and mother .

Advantages for Baby

1. It is a wholesome food for the baby as it contains all the nutrients that a baby needs in first 6 months of life for optimum growth and development .

Proteins : Human milk has low protein (0.7gm / dl) than cow's milk (3.5g / dl) which lowers the solute load on kidneys of baby . Also human milk protein mainly (lactalbumin) is more easily digested than cow's milk protein (Casein) . • **Fat** : Higher content of mono unsaturated fatty acids especially linoleic acid in human milk promotes brain growth and protects individuals from atherosclerosis in later life .

Minerals : Human milk contains a smaller but more balanced proportion of calcium and phosphorous as compared to cow's milk

.

2. **Lowers Risk of Infection**

Human milk contains high level of lysozyme and IgA which offers protection to the baby against several viral and bacterial diseases . Breast milk especially colostrum contains numerous host defense factors like macrophages , granulocytes , T and B lymphocytes . Lactoferrin present in breast milk protects the baby from enteric infections . Para - amino benzoic acid (PABA) present in breast milk protects the baby from malaria .

Protects From Allergy

Higher concentration of secretory IgA in breast milk lowers the risk of milk allergy to the baby so it is the safest food for the baby

4.Therapeutic Effect

Breast feeding protects the baby from E. coli infection due to high levels of bifidus factor in it . Lactoferrin present in breast milk protects the baby from enteric infections . It protects the baby from neonatal hypocalcaemia and tetany (due to its ideal calcium and phosphorous ratio) . Also , exclusively breast fed infants are at lower risk of developing diabetes mellitus , childhood lymphomas , liver diseases and bronchial asthma later in life .

5 . Physiological Adaptation

Mother's milk is very suitable for the baby . Milk of mother who has delivered a preterm baby is different from milk of term baby's mother . Preterm mother's milk contains more energy , protein , fat , sodium , zinc , anti - infective factors and macrophages and has lower lactose , calcium and phosphorous content .

6 . Economic Factors

Breast milk is available free of cost for the baby . Also it is safe and free from any contamination so there is no risk of infection to the baby . This ultimately reduces the cost of hospitalization and economic burden of illness on family .

7 . Emotional Bonding

Breast feeding promotes emotional and physical bonding between the mother and the baby . This leads to better child and mother relationship and fewer behavioral problems in children .

B. Advantages for Mother

1. Lactation suppresses ovulation in mothers who give exclusive breast feeding to their infants and serves as a natural contraceptive .

2 . Breast feeding lowers the risk of ovarian and breast cancer .

3 . Breast feeding is convenient for the mother as she is not required to clean the bottle and prepare milk whenever she feeds the baby .

4. Breast feeding the baby helps mother lose extra weight that she had put during pregnancy .

5. Breast feeding promotes involution of uterus , thus brings back the mother in shape after delivery.

Q 8. Factors Inhibiting Breast Feeding

The following factors may inhibit breast feeding

1. **Psychological Factors**

Shock , strong pain , anger , anxiety or worry can affect let down reflex . So the mother should be encouraged and supported to be calm , relaxed and have a positive attitude while breast feeding .

1. **Early Breast Engorgement**

During and immediately after delivery , breast may be felt full and uncomfortable . Some mothers Maget hard , engorged and painful breast which makes feeding the baby difficult . This problem can be solved by application of warm compress to breast and then expressing excess milk .

3. **Flat and Inverted Nipples**

If the nipples are flat , it is difficult for the baby to get hold of nipple and pull it into the mouth so sucking is interrupted . To overcome this , the flat or inverted nipple may be pulled outward with fingers to stimulate erection . After erection of nipple , baby can be gently put to breast . If not successful , nipple shield may be used .

4 .Sore Nipple

Nipples may be sore because of faulty sucking technique such as baby taking an insufficient amount of areola into mouth while feeding . Nipples may become sore due to long periods of vigorous sucking , sucking in bad position , engorged breast and oral thrush of baby . This can be prevented by teaching the mother about proper breast feeding technique during antenatal period . Mothers should decrease the length of feeding and increase the frequency of feeding . Also mothers should avoid the use of soap on breast as it causes drying . Any emollient like vaseline or edible oil should be applied on the nipples after feeding the baby ,

Q 9 . Complementary Fedding Or Weaning .

= **Definition**

Complementary feeding or weaning is the process of giving an infant other foods and liquids along with breast - milk after the age of 6 months as breast milk alone is no longer sufficient to meet the nutritional requirements of growing baby. It is the process by which the infant gradually becomes accustomed to adult diet.

Guiding Principles for Complementary Feeding

Breast milk alone is not sufficient to meet the nutritional requirements of the baby after 6 months . Also infants are developmentally ready to take other foods at about 6 months . By 6-8 months teeth eruption begins and the baby learns to bite and chew .. The digestive system becomes mature enough to digest starch , protein and fat in non - milk diet . Very young infants push food out with their tongue , but by the age of 6-9 months they are able to hold food in their mouths . Hence , 6 months is the recommended age for weaning .

The energy needed in addition to breast milk is about 200K.cal/ day in infants of 6-8 months , 300 K.cal/day during 9-11 months and 550 K.cal/day during 12-23 months of age . So baby needs extra food in addition to breast milk .

Principle 1 : Practice exclusive breast feeding from birth up to 6 months of age and introduce complementary foods after 6 months of age along with breast feeding .

Principle 2 : Continue frequent on - demand breast feeding until 2 years of age or beyond .

Principle 3 : Practice responsive (active) eding applying the principles of psychosocial care . Feed infants slowly and patiently and encourage them to eat but do not force them . If the child refuses to eat any food , experiment with different food combinations , tastes and textures . Minimize distractions during meals if the child loses interest easily .

Principle 4 : Practice good hygiene and proper food handling to reduce the risk of diarrhea .

Principle 5 : Start at 6 months of age with small amounts of food and increase the quantity as the child gets older , while maintaining frequent breast feeding .

Principle 6 : Gradually increase food consistency and variety as the infant grows older , adapting to the infant's requirements and abilities . Begin liquids at 6 months . By 8 months he can eat semi - solids and by 12 months he can eat solid foods as consumed by rest of the family members .

Principle 7 : Increase the number of times the child is fed complementary food , as the child gets older . A breastfed infant who is 6-8 months old needs 2-3 meals a day and at 9-23 months he needs 3-4 meals a day .

Principle 8 : Feed a variety of nutrient rich foods to ensure that all nutrient needs are met . Complementary foods should provide sufficient energy , protein , vitamins , iron and micronutrients . Complementary food should include animal products , dairy products , pulses , fruits , vegetables and oils .

Principle 9 : Give micronutrient rich complementary foods or vitamin and mineral supplements to the infant as needed .

Principle 10 : It is advisable to start one or two teaspoons of new food at first which should be given when baby is hungry , just before regular feeding , during day time . It may be continued for a few days until the child gets used to the same . Then the new food item may be started , one at a time .

Weaning Foods

Examples of weaning foods that may be started according to the child's ability to feed are :

1. **Liquids** : Soup of vegetables , pulses , rice water and fruit juices .

2. **Semi Solids** : Mashed potato , pulses , boiled vegetables , mashed banana , soft cooked rice and fish .

3 . **Solids** : Cooked rice , chapati , idli , bread , biscuits , groundnuts , banana and fruits .

Problems during Weaning

Several problems may be encountered during weaning , which are as follows

i . If on starting weaning , breast feeding is stopped suddenly , it can have adverse psychological effect on the child .

ii . Weaning food , if prepared unhygienically or not digested properly can cause diarrhea .

iii . If weaning foods are not nutrient rich , the child can develop malnutrition .

iv . Children may develop indigestion , abdominal pain , diarrhea or rashes if they are allergic to certain foods .

Q 10 BFHI

= The Healthy C BABY FRIENDLY HOSPITAL INITIATIVE Baby friendly hospital Initiative (BFHI) was launched jointly by WHO and UNICEF in March 1992 in order to encourage and promote exclusive breast feeding .

Bottle feeding is the biggest killer of babies so BFHI was launched to resurrect the dwindling practice of breast feeding . BFHI aims at improving the knowledge , attitude and practices of health care workers by providing them with knowledge and skills to promote exclusive breast feeding among infants upto the age of 6 months .) The following ten steps are recognized as minimum global criteria for attaining the status of a Baby Friendly Hospital .

Step -1 : Have a written breast feeding policy that is routinely communicated to all health staff . A written policy consisting of ten steps for successful breast feeding should be displayed in the maternal and child health area of the hospital . The policy statement should be available both in english and local language .

Step 2 : Train health care staff in skills necessary to implement this policy . The health care staff should get practical training to implement ten steps of breast feeding . They should be taught the skills needed to assist the nursing mothers for expression of breast milk , correct positioning and attachment of baby during breast feeding .

Step 3 : Inform all pregnant women about the benefits and management of breast feeding . During antenatal period mothers should be informed and educated about the advantages of breast feeding for both mother and baby . The problems like retracted

, small or cracked nipples should be managed during antenatal period .

Step 4 : Help mothers to initiate breast feeding within half - hour of birth . UNIT Establish mother - baby bonding soon after delivery and encourage all mothers to initiate breast feeding within half hour of birth . Mothers should be advised not to administer pre - lacteal feeds .

Step 5 : Show mothers how to breast feed and how to maintain lactation if they are separated from their infants . Mothers should be taught the art of breast feeding including position and technique of feeding . They should be taught the correct technique of expression of breast milk manually or with the help of breast pump , in order to maintain adequate lactation .

Step 6 : Give newborn infants no food or drink other than breast milk , unless medically indicated . No pre - lacteal feeds should be given to the newborn . Only breast feeding should be given . In case breast milk is not available supplementary feeding is given .

Step 7 : Practice rooming - in and allow mothers and infants to remain together round the clock . Keeping mother and newborn together promotes bonding between mother and baby and also helps in timely initiation of breast feeding .

Step 8 : Encourage breast feeding on demand . Mothers should breast feed the babies whenever they are hungry and not according to the clock

Step 9 : Give no artificial feeds or pacifiers to the baby . Pacifiers should not be given to babies due to the risk of infection and non - nutritive sucking . Expressed breast milk or any other medically indicated fluid should be administered through Katori / spoon or palady but not feeding bottle .

Step 10 : Foster the establishment of breast feeding support groups and refer mothers to them on discharge from hospital . Women breast feeding support group should be established in the community for promotion of breast feeding . Follow up support for all breast feeding mothers is necessary after they are discharged from the hospital . The

BFHI movement is active in India under a National Task Force comprising of Government of India , UNICEF , WHO , Voluntary organizations and many professional bodies .

Q 11. Breast feeding, importance, advantages.

= **Advantages of Breast Feeding**

Breast feeding is ideal for the neonates . It has several advantages both for the baby and mother .

Advantages for Baby

1. It is a wholesome food for the baby as it contains all the nutrients that a baby needs in first 6 months of life for optimum growth and development .

Proteins : Human milk has low protein (0.7gm / dl) than cow's milk (3.5g / dl) which lowers the solute load on kidneys of baby . Also human milk protein mainly (lactalbumin) is more easily digested than cow's milk protein (Casein)

Fat : Higher content of mono unsaturated fatty acids especially linoleic acid in human milk promotes brain growth and protects individuals from atherosclerosis in later life .

Minerals : Human milk contains a smaller but more balanced proportion of calcium and phosphorous as compared to cow's milk .

2 . Lowers Risk of Infection Human milk contains high level of lysozyme and IgA which offers protection to the baby against several viral and bacterial diseases . Breast milk especially colostrum contains numerous host defense factors like macrophages , granulocytes , T and B lymphocytes . Lactoferrin present in breast milk protects the baby from enteric infections . Para - amino benzoic acid (PABA) present in breast milk protects the baby from malaria .

3 . Protects From Allergy

Higher concentration of secretory IgA in breast milk lowers the risk of milk allergy to the minibaby so it is the safest food for the baby .

4 . Therapeutic Effect

Breast feeding protects the baby from E. coll infection due to high levels of bifidus factor in it . Lactoferrin present in breast milk protects the baby from enteric infections . It protects the baby from neonatal hypocalcaemia and tetany (due to its ideal calcium and phosphorous ratio) . Also , exclusively breast fed infants are at lower risk of developing diabetes mellitus , childhood lymphomas , liver diseases and bronchial asthma later in life .

5 . Physiological Adaptation

Mother's milk is very suitable for the baby . Milk of mother who has delivered a preterm baby is different from milk of term baby's mother . Preterm mother's milk contains more energy , protein , fat , sodium , zinc , anti - infective factors and macrophages and has lower lactose , calcium and phosphorous content .

6 . Economic Factors

Breast milk is available free of cost for the baby . Also it is safe and free from any contamination so there is no risk of infection to the baby . This ultimately reduces the cost of hospitalization and economic burden of illness on family .

7 . Emotional Bonding

Breast feeding promotes emotional and physical bonding between the mother and the baby . This leads to better child and mother relationship and fewer behavioral problems in children .

B. Advantages for Mother

1. Lactation suppresses ovulation in mothers who give exclusive breast feeding to their infants and serves as a natural contraceptive .

2. Breast feeding lowers the risk of ovarian and breast cancer .

3 . Breast feeding is convenient for the mother as she is not required to clean the bottle and prepare milk whenever she feeds the baby .

4 . Breast feeding the baby helps mother lose extra weight that she had put during pregnancy .

5. Breast feeding promotes involution of uterus , thus brings back the mother in shape after delivery .

Q 12. UNDER - FIVE'S CLINIC

= The concept of under - five's clinic is derived from the Well Baby clinic of the west , for comprehensive health care of children below five years of age . This clinic provides preventive services along with health supervision , treatment , nutritional surveillance and health education .

The services are economical within available resources for a large numbers of young children .

Under - five age groups are vulnerable and special risk group constituting a major portion of total population with high death rate .

The important causes of morbidity and mortality of this group are mainly , ARI , diarrhea , neonatal and perinatal diseases , infections and accidents . These conditions are mostly preventable with adequate health care . This age group also needs regular monitoring for growth and development .

For these reasons , the under - five age group children are provided with special health care through this clinic services .

The services provided by the clinic are set out in the symbol , which has been proposed for under - fives clinics in India.

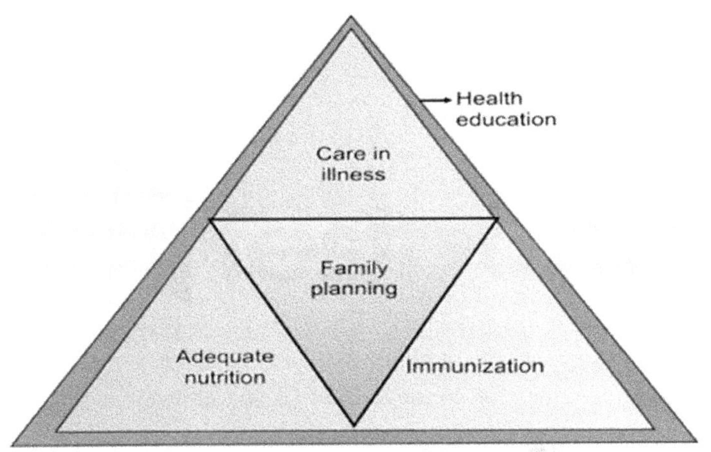

UNDER - FIVE'S CLINIC

The apex of the large triangle represents care in illness , the left triangle represents adequate nutrition , the right triangle represents immunization and the central red triangle represents family planning . The line bordering the big triangle represents health teaching to the mother .

Care in Illness

The care of illness for children provided in the under - 5 clinics includes the followings :

Diagnosis and treatment of :

a . Acute illness , e.g. oral rehydration therapy .

b . Chronic illness including physical , mental , congenital and acquired abnormalities .

c . Disorders of growth and development .

2 . X - ray and laboratory services .

3. Referral services .

Adequate Nutrition

Adequate nutrition is vital for growth and development of children . The health worker should ensure about adequate breastfeeding , weaning and balanced diet of the under - 5 children . Almost all nutritional disorders like PEM , anemia , rickets , nutritional blindness occur in this age group .

Attempts to be made to identify early onset of growth failure and malnutrition . One of the basic activities of the under - fives clinic is growth monitoring . It is done by weighing the child periodically at monthly intervals during the first year , every 2 months during the second year and every 3 months thereafter up to the age of 5 to 6 years .

Food supplementation or on - site feeding are often an integral part of intervention strategies . The ICDS projects has taken up the supplementary feeding of children below 6 years of age .

Nutrition education to the mothers is an important aspect of the clinic .

Immunization

Immunization of six killer diseases , viz . tuberculosis , diphtheria , pertussis , tetanus , poliomyelitis and measles , are administered as per national immunization schedule recommendation . The health worker should motivate and promote the immunization acceptance to prevent morbidity , mortality and disability hazards by these six killer diseases .

Family Planning

The family planning program is successfully conducted through these clinics . The mothers attending the clinic receive counseling with different aspects of family planning practices , which is a significant concern for the health and well - being of the child .

Health Education Health education to the mother is an essential and com pulsory activity of the under - fives clinic . The mothers should receive the information on various aspects of child careand child rearing practices . Preventive measures against malnutrition , ARI , diarrhea tuberculosis , worm infestations , etc. should be informed to the mothers to improve awareness about the disease and its prevention .

The under - fives clinic is usually located in village or a slum or a labor colony . It is managed by trained health worker . She also visits home to educate the mothers and to make sure that children are brought to the clinic for regular check - up . She maintains child registers and records related to child care given and health check - up done . She distributes supplementary food , vitamin ' A ' oil and iron - folic acid tablets and keep accounts of expenditure . She arranges health exhibitions , well - baby competitions and mother craft training program . Thus , ' under- fives ' clinics provide a low cost comprehensive care through preventive promotive , curative and rehabilitative health care services to the under five children .

Q 13. National immunization schedule

=

National Immunization Schedule

for PREGNENT WOMEN

Vaccine	When to give	Dose	Diluent	Route	Site
TT-1	Early in pregnancy	0.5 ml	NO	Intramuscular	Upper Arm
TT-2 #	4 weeks after TT-1	0.5 ml	NO	Intramuscular	Upper Arm
TT-Booster#	If received TT doses in a pregnancy within the last 3 yrs.	0.5 ml	NO	Intramuscular	Upper Arm

for INFANTS

Vaccine	When to give	Max. Age	Dose	Diluent	Route	Site
BCG ##	At birth as early as possible	Till one year of age	0.1 ml (0.05 ml until 1 month age)	Sodium Chloride	Intra-dermal	Left Upper Arm
Hepatitis B Birth Dose ###	At birth as early as possible	within 24 Hours	0.5 ml	NO	Intramuscular	Anterolateral side of mid-thigh LEFT
OPV-0*#	At birth as early as possible	within the first 15 days	2 drops	NO	Oral	-
OPV 1, 2 & 3	At 6, 10 & 14 weeks	Till 5 years of age	2 drops	NO	Oral	-
Rota Virus Vaccine*	At 6, 10 & 14 weeks	Till 1 year of age	5 drops	NO	Oral	-
IPV (Inactivated Polio Vaccine)	At 6 & 14 weeks	Up to 1 yr. of age	0.1 ml	NO	Intradermal	Right Upper Arm
Pentavalent** 1, 2 & 3	At 6, 10 & 14 weeks	Till one year of age	0.5 ml	NO	Intramuscular	Anterolateral side of mid-thigh LEFT
Measles - 1st Dose	9 - 12 completed months	Given till 5 yr of age	0.5 ml	Sterile Water	Subcutaneous	Right Upper Arm
Japanese Encephalities 1st dose	9 - 12 completed months	Till 15 yrs.	0.5 ml	Phosphate Buffer	Subcutaneous	Left Upper Arm
Vitamin A (1st Dose)	At 9 completed months with measles	Till 5 years of age	1 ml (1 lakh IU)	NO	Oral	-

for CHILDREN

Vaccine	When to give	Max. Age	Dose	Diluent	Route	Site
DPT Booster - 1	16-24 months	7 years	0.5 ml	NO	Intramuscular	Anterolateral side of mid-thigh LEFT
Measles 2nd dose	16-24 months	Till 5 years of age	0.5 ml	Sterile Water	Subcutaneous	Right upper Arm
OPV Booster	16-24 months	Till 5 years of age	2 drops	NO	Oral	-
Japanese Encephalities 2nd dose	16-24 months	-	0.5 ml	Phosphate Buffer	Subcutaneous	Left Upper Arm
Vitamin A (2nd to 9th dose)	16 months. Then, 1 dose every 6 months	Till 5 years of age	2 ml (2 lakh IU)	NO	Oral	-
DPT Booster - 2	5-6 years	7 years	0.5 ml	NO	Intramuscular	Upper Arm (Left)
TT	10 years & 16 years		0.5 ml	NO	Intramuscular	Upper Arm

National immunization schedule

Q 14 . Cold chain of vaccines.

= The ' cold chain ' is a system of storage , transport and distribution of vaccines in the state of efficacy and potency at recommended temperature from the manufacturer to the actual recipient of the vaccine .

The failure of cold chain system may lead to ineffective protection against the vaccine preventable diseases . Maintenance of cold chain is the corner stone for the success of immunization program .

All vaccines must be stored , transported and distributed at the recommended temperature by the manufacturer in the literature accompanying the vaccine , otherwise they may become denatured and totally ineffective with loss of potency . For successful cold chain system , three elements are essential , i.e. cold chain equipment , transportation system and motivation and training of the workers for maintenance of cold chain link .

Among all vaccines , polio is the most heat sensitive , requiring storage at -20 ° C . Polio and measles vaccines must be stored in the freezer compartment . DPT , DT , TT , BCG , Typhoid and diluents of vaccines must be stored in the cold part and never allowed to freeze . Vaccines must be protected from sunlight and contact of antiseptic . At the health centers , most vaccines , except polio , can be stored at 4 to 8 ° C for 5 weeks .

Multidose opened vial , which is not used fully must be discarded , within one hour , if no preservative is present . It should be discarded within 3 hours or at the end of a session when preservative is used . Necessary instruction for the particular vaccine must be followed regarding maintenance of required temperature . Instruction for maintenance of vaccine vial monitor (VVM) especially for oral polio vaccine should be followed strictly .

Cold Chain Equipment The cold chain equipments consist the following :

Walk in Cold Rooms

In the regional level , vaccines are stored for 4 to 5 districts in the walk in cold rooms (WIC) , at recommended temperature upto 3 months .

Deep Freezers

Deep freezer is a top opening cold chain equipment and available as 300 liters or 140 liters capacity . Big deep freezer .

Ice lined refrigerator

Cold boxes

Vaccine Carrier

Day carriers

Ice packs

Q 14. Define play & Types of play .

= PLAY

Just as adults work , so does the child plays . It is the main business of the child . Through play the child grows , develops , leams and ultimately matures . Play is the child's daily work .

Definition

Play is an activity in which anyone is engaged for enjoyment without considering its end results .

Types of Play

There are different types of play suitable for young children . Basically all types of play can be categorized into two :

a . Active play

b . Passive play

Active play means children get enjoyment from what they do , where as in passive play children get enjoyment from watching or listening to someone . Passive play is also known as amusement .

Types of Active Play

i . Exploratory Play : A young child's first interest in play is exploratory . The child looks at a toy , shakes it , pounds it to see what noise it makes , sucks it , smells it and squeezes it to see how it feels . Young children enjoy these exploratory activities . They also learn things that they can leam in no other way except play .

ii . Construction : By the time a child is 3 years old , he is no longer satisfied with exploring toys . Children of this age want to use toys to make things . Instead of throwing or biting the blocks , these young ones use them to build towers , bridges , train etc. fit .

iii. Dramatic Play : Just about the time , young children begin to use toys to construct things ; they discover that it is fun to dramatize with toys . To these young children , a doll is not just a doll ; it can be a teacher , mother or a woman . A toy phone can be used to call and talk with someone . With a few articles and clothing , children can quickly turn into any character of drama .

iv Family Games : Before the babies are 2 years of age , they like to play simple games with family members . These games have very few rules and are usually played with any of the family member . The traditional family games for babies are peek - aa - boo , ' Guess which hand ? ' , finding a hidden object etc.

v. Neighbourhood Games : By the age of 4-5 years , children begin to lose interest in family games . Now they want to play with children of their own age . These children are usually from neighborhood . These games are little more complicated then family games.

Types of Passive Play

The enjoyment comes from watching or listening others . Amusement is ideal when the child is tired and yet needs something to avoid boredom and restlessness .

Passive play is of following types :

i . Watching Others : No matter how simple an activity is , young children are fascinated by watching people do it . They like to watch parents and other adults do things in house . Watching others help children learn how to do things and lean new meanings .

ii. Looking at pictures : Bright colored pictures in books , comics , magazines and newspapers greatly appeal young children . Besides enjoyment that they get from looking at picture , they also learn new words and meanings . They learn to associate words with their meaning .

iii . Listening Stories

Q 15. Advantage / Benefits of Play

= **Advantage / Benefits of Play**

i . Sensory Motor Development :

Sensory motor activity is a major component of play at all ages . It has the following benefits :

- It serves as outlet for extra energy .
- It helps in muscle development .
- It gives the child a chance to learn body control .
- It helps the child develop hand and eye co - ordination .
- It helps children to learn increasingly complex and coordinated activities such as race , games , roller skating , bicycle riding etc.

ii . Intellectual Development :

- Through play children develop the ability to keep the mind on task at hand .
- Play gives children a chance to discover meaning of things in the environment .
- Through play children learn about colors , shapes , sizes , textures etc. Play helps children to develop an understanding of abstract concepts and spatial relationships such as up , down , under , over etc.
- Play helps children to differentiate between fantasy and reality .
- It helps in language development .

iii .. Social Development

- Play helps children in socialization . Through play they learn to make friends and get along with others .
- Play gives children a chance to learn to be a good sport a good loser or winner

- It helps children learn the acceptable standards and norms of the society .
- It helps children in learning to take responsibility of their actions .

Iv .Creativity

- Play encourages creativity in children .
- Play gives children an opportunity to experiment and try out their ideas through all the available things like clay , clothes etc.

V .Therapeutic Value

- **Play** provides a way to get rid of anger , fear , jealousy and grief .
- It is a means for release of stress and tension .
- It increases appetite .
- It leads to healthful sleep Through play , children are able to communicate their needs , fears and desires that they are unable to express with their limited language skills .

vi . Moral Value

- Though children learn at home and school those behaviors considered right or wrong , the interaction with peers during play contribute significantly to their moral training .
- To maintain a place in the play group children learn to conform to the standards of the group .
- Through play , children learn acceptable behaviors like fairness , honesty , self - control , tolerance etc.

Q 16 Explain Selection of Toys.

= Selection of Toys Play things or toys should be provided on the basis of child's age , personality , abilities , interest as well as safety

. While buying toys for children , parents must keep in mind the child's physical , intellectual and emotional abilities . Toys should be challenging or should offer problem solving opportunities , but children must be old enough to master the skills required to play with them . Toys should teach new skills and leave room for children to use their imaginations .

While selecting toys for children , parents should keep in mind the following :

1 . Toys should not have sharp edges that can cut .

ii . Toys should not have sharp points that can puncture .

iii . Toys should not have propelling parts that can injure eyes .

iv . Toys should not have small parts that children can swallow or inhale . For children under 3 years of age , any toy or part of toy that is smaller than 1.25 inches in diameter and 2.25 inches in depth is dangerous and should not be given .

V. For infants avoid toys with strings that are 7 inches or longer , since they may cause strangulation .

vi . Toys that produce excessive noise should be avoided as they can cause hearing loss .

vil . Select toys that are light enough and will not cause any harm even if they fall on the child .

viii . Make sure that materials used in toys are non - toxic .

ix . For all children less than 8 years , avoid electric toys .

X. Select toys that are durable enough to survive rough handling by children .

xi . Avoid toys made up of glass . Children must be taught about correct use of toys . Also they must be instructed about maintenance and storage of their toys .

Q 17. PLAY THERAPY

= **Introduction**

Play therapy is generally employed with children aged 3-11 years . It provides a way to them for expression of their experiences and feelings through a natural and self guided process .

Definition

Play therapy is a form of counseling or psychotherapy that uses play to communicate with children and help them to resolve psychosocial challenges . It can also be defined as a technique whereby the child's natural means of expression i.e. play , is used as a therapeutic method to assist him / her in coping with emotional stress or trauma .

Types of Play Therapy

Play therapy can be conducted following different schedules which are as follows :

1 . Individual versus Group Play Therapy : Individual play therapy is useful to cater special requirements of each child . In this type , the play therapist's attention is focused on one child only , to help him solve his problems . Some children do not respond well with Individual play therapy as their problems are of such a nature e.g. shyness , where Individual Play therapy might be difficult . For such children , Group Play Therapy is used where other children are utilized to draw the child out of his problems .

2. Spontaneous or Free Versus Controlled or Situational Play Therapy : In spontaneous play therapy , the child is free to decide what toys he wants to play with , the mode of play , expression of emotions and interaction with play therapists and those around him . This form of therapy is very useful in aggressive children . In controlled play therapy , the child is provided with a situation or setting and his reactions in that situation are noted . This form of therapy gives the child a chance to reflect his conflicts through the characters that he plays in given play situation .

3. Structured Versus Unstructured Play Therapy : In Structured Play Therapy planned situations are used to obtain information about child's behavior . In unstructured play therapy no situation is set and no plans are followed , the child is left free to play .

4. Directive Versus Non - directive Play Therapy : In Directive play therapy , the play therapist sets directions for the child to play . The play therapist makes suggestions and interpretations of the child's words and actions . In non - directive play therapy , the child receives no directions from the therapist . The child is allowed to play according to his own wish .

Play Therapy Team

Many people in health team serve as play therapy team like :

- Child psychologist
- Trained play leader
- Child specialist or pediatrician.
- Nurse.
- Social worker or Counsellor .

CHAPTER THREE

Nursing Care of Neonate

Short answer questions:-

Q 1. APGAR scoring

= Apgar is a quick test performed on a baby at 1 and 5 minutes after birth. The 1-minute score determines how well the baby tolerated the birthing process. The 5-minute score tells the health care provider how well the baby is doing outside the mother's womb.

In rare cases, the test will be done 10 minutes after birth.

The Apgar test is done by a doctor, midwife, or nurse. The provider examines the baby's:

- **Breathing effort**
- **Heart rate**
- **Muscle tone**
- **Reflexes**
- **Skin color**

Each category is scored with 0, 1, or 2, depending on the observed condition.

Breathing effort:

- If the infant is not breathing, the respiratory score is 0.
- If the respirations are slow or irregular, the infant scores 1 for respiratory effort.

- If the infant cries well, the respiratory score is 2.

Heart rate is evaluated by stethoscope. This is the most important assessment:

- If there is no heartbeat, the infant scores 0 for heart rate.
- If heart rate is less than 100 beats per minute, the infant scores 1 for heart rate.
- If heart rate is greater than 100 beats per minute, the infant scores 2 for heart rate.

Muscle tone:

- If muscles are loose and floppy, the infant scores 0 for muscle tone.
- If there is some muscle tone, the infant scores 1.
- If there is active motion, the infant scores 2 for muscle tone.

SCORE	**0 points**	**1 point**	**2 points**
Appearance (Skin color)	Cyanotic / Pale all over	Peripheral cyanosis only	Pink
Pulse (Heart rate)	0	<100	100-140
Grimace (Reflex irritability)	No response to stimulation	Grimace or weak cry when stimulated	Cry when stimulated
Activity (Tone)	Floppy	Some flexion	Well flexed and resisting extension
Respiration	Apneic	Slow, irregular breathing	Strong cry

APGAR scoring

Grimace response or reflex irritability is a term describing response to stimulation, such as a mild pinch:

- If there is no reaction, the infant scores 0 for reflex irritability.
- If there is grimacing, the infant scores 1 for reflex irritability.
- If there is grimacing and a cough, sneeze, or vigorous cry, the infant scores 2 for reflex irritability.

Skin color:

- If the skin color is pale blue, the infant scores 0 for color.
- If the body is pink and the extremities are blue, the infant scores 1 for color.
- If the entire body is pink, the infant scores 2 for color.

Q 2. Kangaroo mother care.

= **Introduction**

Caring low birth weight baby is a great challenge for the neonatal care unit and the family . Number of low birth weight baby is still far beyond the expected target in our country .

The cost of quality management of these babies is increasing day by day . Kangaroo mother care is a low cost approach for the care of low birth weight baby

Definition

Kangaroo mother care (KMC) is a special way of caring low birth weight (LBW) infants by skin - to - skin contact.

It promotes their health and welling by effective thermal control , breastfeeding and bonding . KMC is initiated in hospital and continued at home . Three important aspects of KMC are kangaroo position , nutrition and follow - up .

Components of KMC

In KMC , the infant is continuously kept in skin - to - skin contact by the mother and breastfed exclusively to the utmost extent . The two components of KMC are :

1. Skin - to - skin contact : Direct , continuous and prolonged skin - to - skin contact is provided between the mother and her baby to promote thermal control

2. Exclusive breastfeeding : Skin - to - skin contact promotes lactation and feeding interaction with exclusive breast feeding for adequate nutrition and to improve desired weight gain .

Benefits of KMC

1. KMC helps in thermal control and metabolism . Prolonged , continuous and direct skin - to - skin contact between mother and neonate provides effective thermal control and reduces risk of hypothermia .

2. KMC results in increased duration and rate of breastfeeding .

3. KMC satisfies all five senses of the infant . Baby feels warmth of the mother through skin - to - skin contact (touch) , listen to mothers voice and heart beat (hearing) , sucks the breast to feed (taste) , smells the mother's odor (olfaction) and makes eye contact with mother's (vision) .

4. During KMC , the baby has more regular breathing and less predisposition to apnea .

5. KMC protects against nosocomial infection and reduces incidence of severe illness including pneumonia during infancy .

6. Daily weight gain is slightly better with KMC , thus duration of hospital stay may be reduced . LBW baby Receiving KMC could be discharged from the hospital earlier than conventional care .

7. KMC facilitates better mother - infant bondage due to significantly less stress during kangarooing than the incubator care of the baby .

8. KMC is one of the best methods of transporting small babies by keeping them in continuous skin - to - skin contact with mother or family members .

9. Mother feels increased confidence , self - esteem , sense of fulfillment and deep satisfaction with KMC . Father feels more relaxed , comfortable and better bonded

10. KMC does not require additional staff compared to incubator care .

Preparation for KMC

Counseling

- Explain the benefits of KMC to the mother and the family members .
- Demonstrate the procedure to the mother gently with patience .
- Answer the questions as asked by the mother and the family members to remove anxiety .
- Allow the mother to interact with someone who have already practicing KMC for her baby .
- Discuss about the procedure to the mother - in - law , husband or any other members of the family .

Mother's Clothing

Mother should wear front - open , light dress , as per local culture . Mother can wear sari - blouse , gown , shawl , etc.

Baby's Clothing

socks , Baby should be dressed with front - open sleeveless shirt , cap , and hand gloves .

Q 3. Essential new-born care

= Assessment of new born as soon as possible after birth .

The purpose of the initial assessment are mainly to assess the need for resuscitation, to ascertain the gestational age , to detect presence of any congenital anomalies or any disorders which may affect the well being of the baby . it should be done at the time / place of birth by the trained birth attendant immediately after delivery of the neonate.

Initial Assessment

The initial assessment of neonate is a very important activity immediately after birth . The most essential assessment is the " **first cry** " . Good cry helps in establishment of satisfactory breathing

. The respiration , heart rate and skin color are the basic criterias which should be evaluated immediately to determine the need for life saving support , i.e. resuscitation .

The physiological status including temperature , degree of consciousness , general level of activity , gross congenital anomalies , presence of birth injury , meconium staining and evidence of shock also need to be ascertained immediately and promptly after birth .

Another significant assessment of the neonate is ' Apgar scoring ' as described by Dr Virginia Apgar . Despite its limitations , it is an useful quantitative assessment of neonate's condition at birth , especially for the respiratory , circulatory and neurological status . Five objective criterias are evaluated at one minute and 5 minutes , after the neonates body is completely born . **The criterias are , respiration , heart rote / minute , muscle tone , reflex irritability and skin color .**

Immediate Basic Care of Neonates

Immediate basic care of the newborn at birth includes maintenance of temperature , establishment of open airway , initiation of breathing and maintenance of circulation . As majority babies cry at birth and take spontaneous respiration , no resuscitation requires at birth in about 95 to 98 percent neonates . These healthy normal neonates need only warmth , breastfeeding , close observation for early detection of problems and protection from infections and injuries .

The baby should not be separated from the mother . After cutting the umbilical cord aseptically , the baby should be kept dried , wrapped with dry warm cloths , examined thoroughly and quickly to assess normal characteristics , to detect congenital malformations or any signs of illness and then put to the mother's breast .

Identification tag to be given to the mother and baby . The sex of the baby is shown to the mother . Recording to be done neatly and accurately about the event of birth of the baby (especially birth date , time , sex , examination findings or presence of any problems , etc.) , in the delivery record sheet . The mother and baby should be transfered to lying - in - ward usually after one hour of observation in the delivery room or when the condition setting . permits . Sick or at - risk neonates need special care in special setting.

Q 5.Immediate management of new-born baby.

= The following care needs to be given to the new born at birth , in the labor room

1 . Deliver the baby on a warm and clean towel .
2 . Establish and maintain a patent airway .
3 . Ensure warmth .
4 . Assessment and documentation of baby's condition .
5 . Care of eyes .
6 . Clamp and cut the cord .
7 . Care of skin .
8 . Administration of vitamin K.
9 . Identification of baby .
10. Transfer of the baby according to level of care required .

1. Receive the baby on a warm , clean and dry towel .

2. Establish and maintain a patent airway- The neonate cries spontaneously at birth . During crying the secretions of mouth and nose are suctioned to clear the airway of mucous and amniotic fluid . If the baby is not crying , gentle tactile stimulation is provided . If the child does not cry even after stimulation , CPR should be given . Suction of baby's mouth and nose should be done using a bulb syringe or mucous trap . Gentle suction should be done to prevent bradycardia , laryngospasm and cardiac arrhythmias from Vagal stimulation .

3. Ensure warmth- In neonates , the heat regulating mechanism is immature . The neonate loses heat due to evaporation , radiation , conduction and convection . To prevent heat loss from the baby following steps should be taken The delivery room should be warm , with temperature of 25-28 ° C . • Dry the infant thoroughly soon after birth using a warm towel . · Place the baby under radiant warmer or over the mother's chest in skin to skin contact with her .

• **4. Assessment and documentation of infant's condition** - At 1 minute and 5 minute of birth Apgar scoring is done and while drying the baby head - to - toe assessment is done to find out any abnormality in the new born .

5. Care of Eyes - The eyes of the neonate are cleaned as soon as the head is delivered using sterile cotton swabs dipped in sterile water . The eyes are cleaned from inner canthus to outer canthus with separate swabs for each eye . Thereafter medicated eye drops should be instilled to protect baby's eyes from bacterial infections that may be contracted during delivery .

6. Care of Cord - The umbilical cord is clamped when the cord pulsation stops as this provides the infant with extra blood from the placenta . The cord is clamped with two clamps and then cut between the clamps leaving about 1 " or 5cm from abdomen of baby . The stump is left without any dressing and it is inspected repeatedly for any bleeding for upto 24 hours . It is observed routinely for any redness , inflammation and discharge till it falls off .

7. Care of Skin - The newborn's skin is delicate so it should be gently wiped off blood , mucous and secretions . No attempt should be made to rub off the protective vernix caseosa . The areas with folds such as neck , axillae , groins and creases at joints require special attention . The practice of giving bath to the baby at the time of birth increases the risk of hypothermia so bathing should be postponed for 48-72 hours or more after birth depending on baby's condition .

8. Administration of Vitamin K - For a few days after birth , the new born is unable to synthesize Vitamin K that is needed for blood clotting so there is a potential problem of abnormal bleeding . Therefore 1mg Vitamin K is administered to the baby intramuscularly .

9. Identification of the Baby - Before the baby is transferred from the labor room , an identification band is placed to baby's wrist , specifying the name of mother , registration number , date and time of birth and baby's sex . Also foot impression of baby is taken for baby's identification . It is important to provide mother an opportunity to see and touch the baby and note the sex before transferring the baby to the nursery .

10. Transfer - All the normal babies are transferred to the mother and nursed along with her in post natal area . This is called rooming - in . Breast feeding should be started within half an hour of birth . However , sick or at risk neonates should be transferred to a Neonate Intensive Care Unit (NICU)

Q 6. Nursing Care for Infant Receiving Phototherapy

= Phototherapy (light therapy) is a way of treating jaundice. Special lights help break down the bilirubin in your baby's skin so that it can be removed from his or her body. This lowers the bilirubin level in your baby's blood .

Baby will need to be in an incubator whilst under photo therapy to keep warm

• The phototherapy unit will be placed over the top of the incubator occasionally more than one unit may be used. This can be switched off when your baby needs to come out to be fed

- Proper covering and shielding of gonad
- Assess skin exposure .
- Proper position .
- Care for the infant under phototherapy
- Assess and adjust thermoregulation device .
- Promoting elimination and skin integrity .
- Hydration
- Assure effective of phototherapy
- provide eye protection Eyes are covered with eye-patches to prevent damage to the retina by the .

- Baby is placed naked 45 cm away from the tube lights in a crib or incubator
- If using closer, monitor temperature of the baby.
- Baby is turned every two hours or after each feed
- During phototherapy, the bilirubin level in your baby's blood will be checked at least once every day. Phototherapy is stopped when the bilirubin level decreases.
- Temperature is monitored every two to four hours.
- Weight is taken at least once a day.
- More frequent breastfeeding or 10-20% extra fluid is provided.
- Urine frequency is monitored daily.
- Serum bilirubin is monitored at least every 12 hours.
- Phototherapy is discontinued if two serum bilirubin values are < 10 mg/dl.
- Baby should spend as much time as possible under the phototherapy lights for it to be most effective, but your baby can come out for feeding or cuddles if he or she is upset.
- Baby will need to have regular (usually daily) blood tests whilst under photo therapy to assess the levels of bilirubin and ensure the phototherapy is effective.
- Promoting infant parent interaction.
- Loss , greenish stool .
- Transient skin rashes.
- Hyperthermia .
- Increasing metabolic rate.
- Dehydration .
- Electrolyte disturbance

Q 7. physiological jaundice.

= Neonatal Jaundice Jaundice is the visible manifestation of hyperbilirubinemia . The clinical jaundice in neonates appear on the face at a serum bilirubin level of 5 mg / dL , whereas in adults , it is diagnosed as little as 2 mg / dL . The yellowish discoloration is first seen on the skin of face , nasolabial folds and tip of nose in the neonates . It is detected by blanching the skin with digital pressure in the natural light . Neonatal jaundice is also termed as icterus neonatorum or as neonatal hyperbilirubinemia .

Almost 60 percent term neonates and about 80 percent preterm neonates have bilirubin level greater than 5 mg / dl in the first week of life and about 6 percent of term babies will have bilirubin levels exceeding 15 mg / dL .

Types of Neonatal Jaundice

a . Physiological jaundice

b . Pathological jaundice .

Physiological Jaundice

Multiple factors are responsible for the physiological jaundice , which commonly found in both term and preterm babies . There is elevation of unconjugated bilirubin concentration due to various reasons in the first week of life .

The possible mechanisms of physiological jaundice are as follows :

a . Increased bilirubin load on hepatic cells due to increased volume of RBCs in polycythemia and reduced life span of fetal RBCs and increased enterohepatic circulation of bilirubin .

b . Defective bilirubin conjugation due to decreased enzymatic activity of uridine diphosphate glucurony ! transferase (UDPG - T) .

c . Defective uptake of bilirubin by the liver from plasma due to decreased ligandin and increased ligandin - binding by other anions .

d . Defective bilirubin excretion due to congenital infection .

Characteristics of physiological jaundice

- It appears in between 30 to 72 hours of age in term babies and in preterm babies may appear earlier but not before 24 hours of age .
- Maximum intensity of jaundice is found on the 4th day in term babies and 5th to 6th day in preterm babies .

- Serum bilirubin dose not exceed 15 mg / dL . 0 sand by 14th dari
- Usually disappears by 7th to 10th day in term babies and by 14th day in preterm babies.
- Subsides spontaneously and no treatment is needed .mother need to encourage for breast feeding for adequate hydration and reassurance.
- My aggravated by premaurity, asphyxia, hypothermia, infections and drugs .

Q 0 . Organization of NICU

= **A. physical facilities**

1. Space
2. Location
3. Floor plan
4. Ventilation
5. Lighting
6. Temperature and humidity.
7. Acoustic characteristics
8. Electric outlets
9. Handling and social
10. Communication ystem

B. ward personnel

C . Equipment

i. Resuscitation equipment
ii. Bag and mask culture
iii. Oxygen and suction facilities
iv. Catheter , syringes and needles .
v. Feeding equipments.
vi. Weighing machie
vii. Thermometer

viii. Oxygen hood
ix. Phototherapy unit
x. Infusion pump

D . laboratory facilities
E . Procedure manual.

Q 8. GRADES OF NEONATAL CARE

= Based on birth weight and gestational age , a three tier system of neonatal care is proposed for developing countries .

Level - l

Care About 80 to 90 percent of neonates require minimal care which can be provided by their mothers with support from family members and under supervision of basic health professionals .

The neonates weighing above 2000 g or having gestational age of 37 weeks or more belong to this category . This care can be given at home , subcenter and primary health centers . Essential perinatal care should be provided as basic care at birth , provision of warmth , maintenance of asepsis and promotion of breastfeeding .

Level - Il

Care Neonates weighing between 1500 to 2000 g or having gestational age of 32 to 36 weeks need specialized neonatal care supervised by trained nursing staff and pediatricians . This intermediate neonatal care should be provided by the equipped district hospitals , teaching institutions and nursing homes .

There should be arrangement of resuscitation procedures , maintenance of thermoneutral environment , intravenous infusion , gavage feeding , photo therapy and exchange blood transfusions . Only 10 to 15 percent of all neonates require this care . It should be available at all hospitals where 1000 to 1500 deliveries take place per year .

Level - III

Care Neonates weighing less than 1500 g or born before 32 weeks of gestation require intensive neonatal care . Only 3 to 5 per cent of all newborn babies need this care by skilled nurses and neonatologists especially trained in neonatal intensive care . Apex institutions or regional perinatal centers equipped with centralized oxygen and suction facilities , incubators , ventilators , monitors and infusion pump , etc. are best suited to provide intensive neonatal care . High - risk pregnancies which are associated with birth of high risk neonates must be identified during pregnancy and referred to an appropriate center for skilled management and better outcome .

At birth , detection of high risk neonates should be done at all levels of health care delivery system and appropriate refferal is essential to different levels of neonatal care for prevention and reduction of neonatal mortality and morbidity.

Q 9. NEONATAL RESUSCITATION

= **Introduction**

Approximately 10 % of newborns require some assistance to begin breathing at birth . Less than 1 % require extensive resuscitation measures / The National Resuscitation Program was developed by American Academy of Pediatrics (AAP) in conjunction with American Heart Association (AHA) following the neonate resuscitation guidelines . According to the National Resuscitation Program , those newborns that do not require resuscitation can generally be identified by a rapid assessment of following 3 characteristics

Term Gestation ?

Crying or Breathing ?

Good muscles tone ?

If answer to all these questions is " Yes " , the baby does not need resuscitation . The baby should be dried and placed in skin - to - skin contact with the mother . Apgar scoring should be done simultaneously . If answer to above three questions is " No " , the infant requires resuscitation .

TABC of Resuscitation

T- Maintenance of Temperature

• Dry the baby quickly .

• Remove wet linen .

• Place the baby under radiant warmer .

A- Establish an open airway

• Position the infant .

• Suction mouth and nose [in few cases also trachea] .

.ET intubation , if needed to ensure open airway .

B - Initiate Breathing

• Tactile stimulation to initiate respiration .

• PPV when necessary , using either Bag and mask or Bag and ET tube

C - Circulation

• Chest compression

• Medications (if needed)

LAQ

A. Define Preterm baby

A.

Characteristics of preterm baby

B.

small for date baby

= Low birth weight Infants

Low birth weight Infants are of two types .

1.Preterm 2. small for date

Define

A baby born before completion of 37th week of gestation, regard less of birth weight.

FEATURES

SPECIFICATION

Size

A preterm baby is small in size, usually less than 47cm and weight less than 2.5 kg.

Posture

The preterm infant lies in a "relaxed attitude", limbs are extended.

Head

The head is relatively large, sutures are widely separated and fontanels are large.

Hair

Hair of preterm are fine, fuzzy and wooly.

Skin

Skin of preterm is thin, pinkish and appears shiny due to generalized edema. It is covered with abundant lanugo and there is little vernix caseosa

Ear

In preterm infants ear cartilage is poorly developed and ear may fold easily.

Breast

The breast nodule is absent or less than 5mm wide.

Sole

The sole of foot of preterm infant appears more turgid and may have only fine wrinkles. The creases are absent

Female genitalia

The female infant's clitoris is prominent and labia majora are poorly developed and gaping

Male genitalia

In preterm male infant, the scrotum is undeveloped and not pendulous, minimal rugae are present and testes may be in the inguinal canal or in the abdominal cavity.

Scarf

sign In preterm infants elbow may be easily brought across chest with little or no resistance.

Heel to Ear maneuver

The preterm infant's heel is easily brought to the ear, meeting with no resistance

small for date baby:

A baby whose birth weight falls below the 10th percentile on intrauterine growth curve is known as small for date or small for gestational age .

Classification of Small-for-date

SFD or SGA babies are of 3 types:

1.Malnourished small-for-date infants:- Growth arrest in later part of pregnancy leads to reduction in cell size but not cell number, resulting in small and malnourished baby. Such baby looks marasmic and has less subcutaneous fat and poor muscle mass.

2. Hypoplastic small-for-date babies:- Growth retardation in early part of pregnancy leads to reduction in number of body cells resulting in hypoplastic small for date babies. These babies are proportionately smaller in all parameters including head size.

3. Mixed:- When adverse factors operate during early and mid pregnancy, reduction in both cell number and size occurs leading to mixed small for date baby.

CHAPTER FOUR

Integrated management of neonatal & childhood illness (IMNCI)

Short answer questions:-

Q 1. IMNCI

= **INTEGRATED MANAGEMENT OF NEONATAL AND CHILDHOOD ILLNESS.**

Over the last 3 decades, the annual number of deaths in children less than 5 years of age, has decreased by almost one third. However this reduction has not been evenly distributed throughout the world. Every year more than 10 million children die in developing countries, before they reach their fifth birthday.

The common causes of infant and child mortality in developing countries like India are perinatal conditions, acute respiratory infections, diarrhea, malaria, measles and malnutrition.

IMNCI Guidelines

The IMNCI clinical guidelines target children less than 5 years - the age group that bears highest burden of deaths due to common childhood diseases. The guidelines take evidence based syndromic approach to case management, that supports rational, effective and affordable use of drugs and diagnostic tools. Evidence based medicine stresses the importance of evaluation of evidence from clinical research and cautions against the use of unsystematic and untested pathophysiologic reasoning for medical decision making. Careful and systematic assessment of common symptoms and well selected clinical signs provide sufficient information to guide rational and effective actions.

An evidence-based syndromic approach can be used to determine:

- Health problem or problems of child
- Severity of child's condition
- Actions that can be taken to care for the child (e.g. refer the child immediately or manage with available resources or manage at home).

IMNCI promotes

i, Adjustment of interventions to the capacity and functions of the health system. ii. Active involvement of family members and community in health care process because parents if correctly informed and counseled, can play an important role in improving health status of the child

Essential Components of IMNCI Strategy

The IMNCI strategy includes both preventive and curative interventions that aim to improve practices in health facilities, the health system and at home. The strategy includes three main components:

a) Improvement in case management skills of health staff through provision of locally adapted guidelines.

b) Improvement in overall health system.

c) Improvement in family and community health care practices.

Principles of Integrated Care

The IMNCI guidelines focus on children upto 5 years of age. The treatment guidelines have been broadly described under two categories :

Young infants age upto 2 months

Children age 2 months to 5 years

The IMNCI Guidelines are based on following principles:

i. All sick young infants age up to 2 months must be examined for signs of "possible serious bacterial infection" and all children of 2months to 5 years must be examined for "general danger signs" which indicate the need for immediate referral or hospitalization.

ii. All sick children be routinely assessed for major symptoms, nutritional and immunization status, feeding problems and other problems.

iii. Only a limited number of specific clinical signs are used to diagnose the diseases.

iv. Based on presence of selected clinical signs, the child is placed in a classification that indicates the severity of condition and treatment required. The classifications are color coded "pink" that suggests referral, "yellow" that indicates initiation of treatment in health facility and "green" indicating home management.

V. IMNCI guidelines address most common, but not all major pediatric problems.

vi. IMNCI procedures use a limited number of essential drugs.

vii. It encourages active participation of caretakers in treatment of children.

viii. IMNCI includes Counseling of caretakers about home care including feeding, fluids and follow up.

IMNCI Case Management Process

The IMNCI case management process includes the following steps:

1. Assess the young infant/child.

2.Classify the illness.

3. Identify the treatment

4. Treat the young infant/child

5. Counsel the mother

6. Provide follow up care

Q 2. IMNCI case management process

= The IMNCI case management process includes the following steps:

1. Assess the young infant/child.
2.Classify the illness.
3. Identify the treatment
4. Treat the young infant/child
5. Counsel the mother
6. Provide follow up care

FOR ALL SICK CHILDREN AGE BIRTH UP TO 5 YEARS WHO ARE BROUGHT TO A FIRST-LEVEL HEALTH FACILITY

↓

ASSESS the child: Check for general danger signs (or possible bacterial infection in the young infant). Ask about main symptoms. If a main symptom is reported, assess further. Check nutrition, HIV and immunization status. Check also for other problems.

↓

CLASSIFY the child's illnesses: Use a colour-coded triage system to classify the child's main symptoms and his or her nutrition or feeding status.

IF URGENT REFERRAL is needed and possible

↓

IDENTIFY URGENT PRE-REFERRAL TREATMENT(S) needed for the child's classifications.

↓

TREAT THE CHILD: Give urgent pre-referral treatment(s) needed.

↓

REFER THE CHILD: Explain to the child's caretaker the need for referral. Calm the caretaker's fears and help resolve any problems. Write a referral note. Give instructions and supplies needed to care for the child on the way to the hospital.

IF NO URGENT REFERRAL is needed or possible

↓

IDENTIFY TREATMENT needed for the child's classifications: Identify specific medical treatments and/or advice.

↓

TREAT THE CHILD: Give the first dose of oral drugs in the clinic and/or advise the child's caretaker. Teach the caretaker how to give oral drugs and how to treat local infections at home. If needed, give immunizations.

↓

COUNSEL THE MOTHER: Assess the child's feeding, including breastfeeding practices, and solve feeding problems, if present. Advise about feeding and fluids during illness and about when to return to a health facility. Counsel the mother about her own health.

↓

FOLLOW-UP care: Give follow-up care when the child returns to the clinic and, if necessary, reassess the child for new problems.

IMNCI case management process

CHAPTER FIVE

Nursing management in common childhood diseases.

A . NUTRITIONAL DEFICIENCY DISORDERS

Short answer questions:-

Q1. Diarrhoea-fluid management.

= DIARRHEA

Introduction

Diarrhea is derived from a Greek word, meaning 'flowing through'. It is a common cause of infant deathsworldwide. It is the second leading cause of death in children under 5 years of age. The loss of fluidsthrough diarrhea can cause dehydration, which if not managed promptly may result in death of the child.

Diarrhea is both treatable and preventable.

Definition

According to the World Health Organization, diarrhea is defined as 'passage of 3 or more loose stools per day or passing more stools than normal for the age'

It is the change in consistency of stools rather than the number of stools that is more important.

Classification

1. On the basis of duration

On the basis of duration for which diarrhea lasts, it is of 2 types:

a. Acute diarrhea: If an episode of diarrhea lasts for less than 14 days, it is known as acute

diarrhea.

b. Chronic Diarrhea: If diarrhea lasts for 14 days or more, it is known as chronic diarrhea.

Management

The management of infants and young children with diarrhea and dehydration focus on:

1. Replacement of the fluids
2. Administration of prescribed drugs
3. Maintenance of nutritional status
4. Prevention of Diarrhea
5. Educating parents

1. Fluid replacement :

Oral rehydration therapy is of prime importance for replacement of lost fluids in dehydrated patients.

Oral rehydration refers to drinking of solution which contains clean water, sugar and mineral salts in order to replace the fluid and electrolytes lost from the body during diarrhea.

Administration of ORS

Oral rehydration solution (ORS) can be used to prevent development of dehydration and in many cases is a life saver. Homemade solutions that can be used for oral rehydration are salted rice water, salted pulses (daal) water, salted yogurt drinks (lassi, chachh), vegetable and chicken soups. At home, ORS can be prepared by mixing in 1 litre water, three finger pinch salt (3 grams) and two tablespoons sugar (18 grams). This solution should be given to the child after every loose stool.

WHO and UNICEF recommended and distributed ORS packets as a drug for treatment of clinical dehydration. In 1984, another mixture containing trisodium citrate instead of sodium bicarbonate was developed, with the aim of improving the stability of ORS in hot and humid climates.

The new ORS has lesser glucose and salt concentration which reduces the possible adverse effects of hypertonicity. The contents of readymade ORS packets are to be dissolved in one litre of clean drinking water.

i. Treatment plan A

This plan is followed for patients without the physical signs of dehydration or having mild dehydration. For children with mild dehydration, mothers are educated to give increased amount of home based fluids to the child, like rice water, salted lassi, lemon water, coconut water, soups, fruit juice, daal water etc. In addition, home made ORS can be prepared and given to the child. The mother should be told to administer ORS after each loose stool in the amount mentioned in table below.

WHO recommends that if the child vomits, wait for five to ten minutes and then start giving the solution again, slowly. Also the mother should be asked to take the child to the physician if the child does not get better within 3 days or if he develops any danger signs of dehydration.

ii. Plan B

This treatment plan is followed for patients with signs of moderate dehydration. These patients need to be treated in a health centre or hospital. The fluid therapy for patients with moderate dehydration has three components –

a. Correction of existing water and electrolyte defect (Rehydration therapy)

b. Replacement of ongoing losses due to continuing diarrhea (Maintenance therapy)

c. Provision of normal daily fluid requirement

iii. Treatment Plan C

This treatment plan is followed for children with severe dehydration. In severe dehydration, start intravenous fluids immediately. Also give ORS if the child can drink. The best IV fluid solution that should be given is Ringer lactate solution. An ideal preparation is Ringer lactate with 5% dextrose. If ringer lactate is not available, normal saline (0.9%) can be used. Any of these solutions should be given in a dose of 100 ml/kg body weight.

Q 2. Vitamin A deficiency and its prevention

= Lack of vit A is called the vitamin A deficiency . it is common in developing countries . Night blindness is the one of the first sign of vitamin A deficiency.

Vtamin A Deficiency

- Breast milk of mothers with vitamin A deficiency contains little vitamin A which provides the breast fed child with too little vitamin A.
- Malabsorption: Infective absorption of vitamin A in the body can also lead to vitamin A deficiency.
- Malnutrition: Inadequateintake of vitamin A in the diet leads to Vitamin A deficiency.
- Zinc deficiency: Deficiency of zinc can impair absorption, transport and metabolism of vitamin A because it is essential for synthesis of vitamin transport proteins.
- Iron deficiency: It can affect vitamin A uptake

Clinical Manifestations of Deficiency

I .Night blindness: There is difficulty for the eyes to adjust to dim light. The affected individuals are unable to distinguish images in low levels of illumination. They have poor vision in dark but can see normally in adequate light. Night blindness caused by Vitamin A deficiency is associated with loss of goblet cells in the conjunctiva of eye.

ii. Xerophthalmia: A condition in which eye fails to produce tears.

iii. Xerosis Conjunctiva: Conjunctiva is dry, thickened, wrinkled and pigmented due to keratinisation of epithelial cells.

iv. Xerosis Cornea: Dryness spreads to cornea.

V. Bitot's spot: Greyish or white plaques formed of desquamated conjunctival epithelium, adhering to conjunctiva.

vi. Keratomalacia: Untreated xerosis of conjunctiva and cornea leads to development of keratomalacia. The corneal epithelium becomes opaque and ulcerated. This leads to bacterial invasion of cornea that results in blindness.

vii. Follicular hyperkeratosis (Phrynoderma): There is hyperkeratinisation of epithelial lining of hair follicles. The skin becomes rough, dry and papules develop on skin.

vill. Growth retardation

ix. Impaired immunity (increased risk of ear infection and urinary tract infection) Vitamin A is required for the proliferation of T-killer cells. A deficiency of Vitamin A suppresses the T cells, thereby causing impaired immunity.

Management

1. **Supplementation**

Mild to moderate cases should be given 10,000µg/daily. Severe cases should get 50,000µg/daily for few weeks

1. **Dietary consumption .**

Consumption of yellow or orange fruits and vegetables which contains carotenoid especially B-carotene is beneficial.

Prevention

i. Vitamin A, Palmitate-A, Aquasol A are the drugs available in market as Vitamin A supplements. These supplements must be given to the children as per physicians order.

ii. Maternal high supplementation benefits both mother and breast fed infant. High dose of vitamin A supplementation to lactating mother in first post-partum month can provide breastfed infant with appropriate amount of vitamin A through breast milk.

iii. Increased consumption of vitamin A rich food of animal origin, in addition to fruits and vegetables is the best way of preventing Vitamin A deficiency.

iv. Diet which is rich in vitamin A should be given to growing children.

V. Reduce frequency and severity of factors contributing to Vitamin A Deficiency. E.g. PEM, Diarrhea and Measles.

vi. Administration of Vitamin A as a part of immunization schedule. vii. Fortification of foods with vitamin A is costly, but can be done in wheat, sugar and milk.

Q 3. Protein energy malnutrition .

= *Protein Energy Malnutrition*

Protein Energy Malnutrition (PEM) is defined as a range of pathological conditions arising from coincident lack of varying proportions of protein and calorie, occurring most frequently in infants and young children and often associated with infection (WHO,1973) PEM affects children under 5 years of age belonging to the poor underprivileged communities.

Under nutrition is a complex condition with multiple deficiencies such as proteins,energy and micro nutrient deficiencies often occurring together. According to WHO, malnutrition is an underlying factor in over 50 % of the 10 – 11 million yearly deaths of children under 5 years.

Classification of PEM

Protein energy malnutrition may be classified into three types as follows:

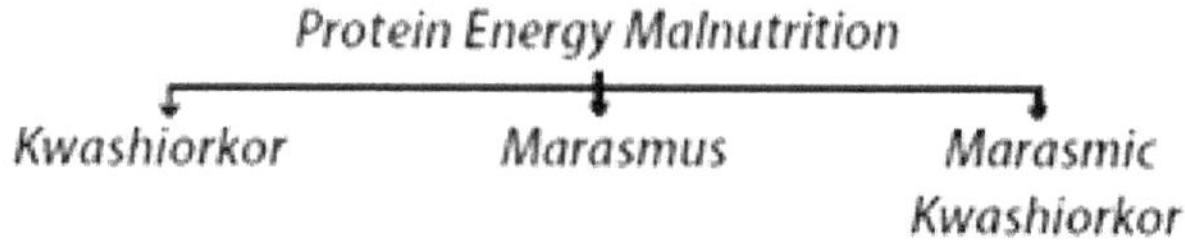

Fig 10.6: Classification of PEM

Classification of PEM

I. Kwashiorkor

Kwashiorkor is due to inadequate protein in the diet despite an adequate calories intake

Children are more affected by kwashiorkor than adult . it typically than adults. It typically starts after the child has breast milk has been replaced by diet with low in protein, although it can occur in infants if the mother is protein deprive .

Kwashiorkor is a form of severe protein malnutrition characterized by edema and an enlarged liver with fatty infiltrates.

It cause by sufficient calories intake but with insufficient protein consumption, which distinguishes it from marasmus.

Clinical signs and symptoms

Growth failure

- Oedema of the face and lower limbs
- Muscle wasting
- Fatty liver
- Anorexia(loss of appetite)
- Diarrhoea
- Change in the colour, sparse, soft and thin hair.
- Change in the colour of the skin(hypo and hyperpigmentation)
- Anaemia
- Vitamin A deficiency

· Angular stomatitis(Cracks in the corners of mouth)
· Cheilosis (inflammation and cracks in lips)
· Moon face

ii. Marasmus

This is caused by severe deficiency of proteins and calories in the diet. The important features are as follows:

Severe wasting of muscles
· Loss of subcutaneous fat (Limbs appear as skin and bones)
· Skin is dry and atrophic
· Anaemia
· Eye lesions due to Vitamin A deficiency
· Irritability and fretfulness
· Diarrhoea
· Dehydration
· Body temperature is sub-normal
· Failure to thrive
· Wrinkled skin - Old man's face
· Grossly underweight

III. Marasmic Kwashiorkor

Children suffering from this disease show signs of both kwashiorkor and marasmus.

Q 4. Kwashiorkor.

= Kwashiorkor is due to inadequate protein in the diet despite an adequate calories intake

Children are more affected by kwashiorkor than adult . it typically than adults. It typically starts after the child has breast milk has been replaced by diet with low in protein, although it can occur in infants if the mother is protein deprive .

Kwashiorkor is a form of severe protein malnutrition characterized by edema and an enlarged liver with fatty infiltrates.

It cause by sufficient calories intake but with insufficient protein consumption, which distinguishes it from marasmus.

Kwashiorkor is occurred in area of famine or poor food supply.

Kwashiorkor is a severe form of malnutrition associated with a deficiency in dietary protein , the extreme lack of protein causes osmotic imbalance in gastro-intesteinal system causing swelling of the gut diagnosis as an edema or retention of water.

Sign and symptoms :

The defining sign of kwashiorkor in a malnourished child is pitting edema. (Swelling of ankles and feet) .

Other signs includes a distended abdomen, an enlarged liver wuth fatty infiltrate , thinning of liver ,loss of teeth , skin depigmentation and dermatitis.

Generally the disease can be treated by adding protein to the diet, however, it can have a long term impact on a child physical and mental development, and in severe cases may leads death.

Q6. Malnutrition.

= Definition of malnutrition : faulty nutrition due to inadequate or unbalanced intake of nutrients or their impaired assimilation or utilization .

Malnutrition occurs when the body doesn't get enough nutrients.

Causes include a poor diet , digestive conditions or another disease .

Malnutrition is a condition that occurs that result from eating a diet in which one more nutrients are not enough or are to much that the diet causes health problems.

It may involve calories , protein, carbohydrates, fat , vitamins, or minerals.

No enough nutrient is called under nutrition or undernourishment while too much is called overnutrition.

Malnutrition is often used to specifically refer to undernoutrishment where an individual is not getting enough calories, proteins, or micronutrients.

If undernutrition occurs during pregnancy,or beforetwo years of age it may results in a permant problems with a physical and mental development.

Extreme undernourishment knows as starvation may have symptoms that include a short height, thin body, very poor energy levels , and swollen legs and abdomen.

People also often get infectious and are frequently cold . The symptom of micronutrients deficiencies depend on the micronutrient deficiencies depend on the micronutrient that is lacking.

Undernourishment is most often due to not enough high quality food being available to eat . this is food being available to eat This is often related to high food price and poverty.

There are two main types of undernutition :

1. **Protein energy malnutrition (PEM)**
2. **Dietary deficiencies .**

1 . Protein energy malnutrition has two severe forms : (a) Marasmus (A lack of protein and calories) (b) Kwashiorkor (A lack of protein)

2 . Dietary deficiencies : A lack of iron , iodine , vitamins, and minerals.

We can beat malnutrition by giving food security to people . Gov to be take a proper actions and efferts to bring modern agricultural techniques to increase food quality and quantity and increases nutrients contains.

Q 7. Difference between kwashiorkor and marasmus.

=

Table 10.5: Differences between Kwashiorkor and Marasmus

Kwashiorkor	Marasmus
It develops in children whose diets are deficient of protein.	It is due to deficiency of proteins and calories.
It occurs in children between 6 months and 3 years of age.	It is common in infants under 1 year of age.
Subcutaneous fat is preserved.	Subcutaneous fat is not preserved
Oedema is present.	Oedema is absent.
Enlarged fatty liver.	No fatty liver.
Ribs are not very prominent.	Ribs become very prominent.
Lethargic	Alert and irritable.
Muscle wasting mild or absent.	Severe muscle wasting
Poor appetite.	Voracious feeder.
The person suffering from kwashiorkor needs adequate amounts of proteins.	The person suffering from marasmus needs adequate amount of proteins, fats and carbohydrates.

B . DISORDERS OF RESPIRATORY SYSTEM .

Long answer questions:-

Q 3. A. Define Bronchopneumonia.

B . Enlist the Causative agents, and clinical features of Bronchopneumonia.

C .Explain the nursing management of patient with Bronchopneumonia

= PNEUMONIA

Definition

Pneumonia is defined as acute inflammation and consolidation of lung parenchyma.

Incidence

Pneumonia in children is a major concern in developing countries, because 1/3rd of all hospital out patients comprise of acute respiratory infections of which nearly 30% have pneumonia. It is the second leading cause of death in children under five years of age.

Classification Pneumonia can be classified on anatomic and etiologic basis.

A. Classification on anatomic basis

a. Lobar or lobular pneumonia: One or more lobes of lungs are involved.

b. Interstitial pneumonia: Interstitial tissues of lungs are affected.

c. Bronchopneumonia: Patchy consolidation of lungs is known as **bronchopneumonia.**

B. Classification on etiologic basis

a. Bacterial pneumonia: It may be caused by Pneumococcus, Streptococcus, Staphylococcus, Hemophilus influenza and H. pertussis.

b. Viral pneumonia: It is caused by viruses like Influenza, Measles, Adenovirus and Respiratory Syncytial Virus.

c. Fungal pneumonia: It may be caused by histoplasmosis and Coccidiomycosis.

d. Protozoal pneumonia: It is caused by Pneumocystis camii, Toxoplasma **gondii and Entamoeba histolytica**

C. Miscellaneous types

a. Aspiration Pneumonia: It is caused by aspiration of food, nasal drops, amniotic fluid by newborn, water (drowning) and chemicals like kerosene oil etc.

b. Loffler's pneumonia: It is a disease in which eosinophils accumulate in lungs, in response to parasitic infection. It may be caused by parasites like Ascaris lumbricoides, Strongyloides stercoralis and Ancylostoma duodenale.

C. Hypersensitivity pneumonitis: It is an inflammation of alveoli within the lungs caused by hypersensitivity to inhaled dust.

d. Hypostatic pneumonia: It results from collection of fluid in dorsal region of lungs and occurs especially in those confined to bed for long time (like bedridden or elderly persons).

Clinical Features

Clinical features of Pneumonia include

- Sudden onset
- High fever with chills
- Cough with thick sputum
- Increased respiratory rate
- Grunting respiration
- Nasal flaring
- Running nose
- Irritability
- Malaise
- Sore throat
- Anorexia

Late Symptoms Include:

- Convulsions
- Drowsiness
- Inability to drink from mouth
- Chest in drowning
- Wheezing
- Hoarseness of voice
- Cyanosis
- Pleural pain which may be increased by deep breathing and is referred to shoulder or abdomen.

Management

Nursing Management

i. Make continuing assessment.

- Monitor the child's respiratory rate and pattern.
- Monitor breath sounds to note presence of rales, ronchi and wheezing.
- Observe for signs of respiratory distress.

ii. Facilitate respiratory efforts.

- Maintain patent airway and provide high humidity atmosphere.
- Administer oxygen to maintain the oxygen saturation in blood.
- Place the child in semi-fowlers position to help in breathing.
- In case of unilateral pneumonia, make the child lie on affected side, to splint the chest wall and prevent painful pleural rubbing.
- Position of the child should be changed frequently to prevent pooling of secretions in lungs.

    - Keep the child warm and comfortable.

- Administer cough suppressants and bronchodilators, as prescribed.
- . Provide steam inhalation and chest physiotherapy to help in drainage of secretions.
- If the child is old enough, teach him effective coughing and deep breathing.
- Give increased amount of fluids as this will help in liquefying the thick tenacious secretions.

iii. Control fever

- Provide bed rest to the child.
- Administer the prescribed antibiotics.
- Tepid sponging is done to reduce fever.
- Increase the fluid intake to prevent dehydration.

iv. Maintain fluid and electrolyte balance along with nutritional status of the child.

- Provide adequate fluids to meet increased fluid demand of the body.
- If the child is having breathing difficulty, do not give anything orally as there is greater risk of aspiration.
- When oral feedings are started, after the child's condition permits, feed the child slowly and carefully to prevent aspiration and aggravation of cough.
- Give high calorie liquid diet to the child.

Promote rest and sleep.

- Handle the child as little as possible to provide rest. Provide diversion therapy to the child to avoid boredom.
- Administer mild sedatives (if prescribed) when the child is restless or irritable.
- Make the baby lie on affected side, to splint the chest wall and reduce pleural pain.
- Administer cough suppressants before the baby sleeps.

Q 4. RESPIRATORY DISTRESS SYNDROME

Introduction

Respiratory distress syndrome of newborn previously called hyaline membrane disease, is a syndrome in premature infants caused by developmental insufficiency of surfactant production and structural immaturity of the lungs.

Respiratory Distress syndrome is the leading cause of death in preterm infants. It occurs in 50% babies born at 26-28 weeks and 25% of babies born at 30-31 weeks. Idiopathic respiratory distress syndrome is an acute disorder that occurs almost exclusively in premature infants.

The syndrome is more frequent in infants of diabetic mothers and those born by cesarean section.

Clinical Features

Respiratory Distress syndrome begins shortly after birth and is manifested by

Tachypnea

Tachycardia

Chest Wall Retractions

Expiratory Grunting

Nasal Flaring and

Cyanosis

As the disease progresses the baby may develop ventilatory failure (rising CO_2 concentration in blood) and prolonged cessation of breathing

Diagnostic Evaluation

i. Physical examination

Most neonates who have Respiratory distress syndrome experience breathing difficulty at birth within 2 hours after birth. Silverman retraction score is a very good method of assessing severity of respiratory distress. The most common sign of abnormal ventilation is tachypnea, a respiratory rate of over 60 breaths /minute. The infant has grunting on expiration. Nasal flaring is also present, which indicates respiratory distress. Auscultation of chest reveals diminished breath sounds. As the baby's condition worsens, bradycardia or tachycardia occurs. Physical examination: These infants are generally flaccid hypoactive and motionless. They assume typical frog-legged position. The neonate may have pallor, oedema, hypothermia and shock like state in severe condition.

ii. Chest x-ray of baby shows areas of atelectasis and an air bronchogram shows air filled bronchi.

iii. Arterial blood gas analysis is done which shows arterial pco_2 above 65mm of Hg (though the normal upper limit is 45mm Hg), an arterial po_2 of 40mm Hg (though the normal limit is 50mm Hg) and PH below 7.15 when normal PH is 7.35-7.45.

iv. Shake test is done on gastric aspirate withdrawn from the neonate in the first hour of life.

v. Prenatal diagnosis of Respiratory distress syndrome can be made by determining lecithin/ sphingomyelin ratio in amniotic fluid. L/S ratio of more than 2 indicates adequate lung maturity.

Management

Respiratory distress is the most common life threatening emergency in premature newborns.

The principles of management of Respiratory distress syndrome include

i. Improving ventilation to enhance oxygenation.

ii. Correction of acidosis

iii. Maintenance of thermo neutral environment

iv. Adequate nutrition

Management of baby with RDS includes:

i. Monitoring of the baby's condition:

- To monitor the baby's condition, following clinical observations are to be done
- Rectal or skin temperature should be noted hourly
- Hourly monitoring of respiratory rate.
- Noting the severity of retraction and grunting.
- Status of peripheral pulse and B.P.
- Skin color
- Apneic episodes
- Activity, responsiveness and cry of the baby.
- Urine output. till stable and thereafter every 4 hourly.

ii. Intravenous infusion for maintaining acid-base balance and nutritional status of baby: It is advisable to start intravenous infusion in all the babies with Respiratory distress syndrome because oral feeding may not be possible with the baby as oral feeding has the risk of aspiration. The infant needs to be given nasogastric feeding or total parenteral nutrition to prevent tissue catabolism. 7.5% soda bicarb should be administered to the baby in dose of 3-8 meq/kg in 24 hours or the dose of soda bicarb may be calculated according to the baby's PH.

iii. Ventilatory support: Infants with hyaline membrane disease are handicapped by decreased lung compliance and alveolar collapse during expiration. Administration of oxygen under positive pressure would prevent alveolar collapse and ensure gas exchange throughout the respiratory cycle. CPAP (Continuous Positive Airway Pressure) is indicated and useful in infants with decreased lung compliance.

iv. oxygen via hood

v. warmth and humidity.

vi. Surfactant therapy .

vii. Antibiotics :

viii. Administration of antibiotics

Nursing Management

i. Preterm with Respiratory distress syndrome should be prevented from infection by using isolation and aseptic precautions.
ii. The critically ill infant should be minimally handled
iii. These infants should be positioned with head elevated, to reduce the pressure on diaphragm.
iv. Airway should be kept patent and opened by extending the head slightly. This can be done by placing a folded sheet or towel under the baby's shoulders.
v. As the baby requires oxygen administration for long duration via face mask or nasal prongs, a soothing antibiotic ointment can be applied to irritated skin surface.
vi. Keep the baby warm by placing the baby in incubator/radiant warmer.
vii. Monitor vital signs regularly.
viii. Endotracheal suctioning should be done as required, using strict aseptic techniques.
ix. Monitor oxygen saturation while suctioning the baby

x. Measure baby's weight daily to assess adequacy of fluid administration.
xi. Administer intravenous fluids/Nasogastric feed and medications as prescribed by the physician.

C .DISORDERS OF GASTROINTESTINAL SYSTEM

Q 5. Explain the disorders of gastrointestinal system

= 1. CONGENITAL DISORDERS OF GASTROINTESTINAL SYSTEM

a. Disorders of mouth

- Cleft lip and cleft palate

b. Disorder of oesophagus

- Tracheo- oesophageal fistula

C. Disorders of stomach

- Pyloric stenosis

d. Disorder of intestine

- Intestinal obstruction
- Hernia
- Intussusception
- Hirschsprung's disease
- Anorectal malformation

II INFECTION AND INFESTATION OF GASTROINTESTINAL SYSTEM

- Diarrhea
- Worm infestation

III MISCELLANEOUS DISORDERS

- Indian childhood cirrhosis
- Fluid and electrolyte crisis

Q6. Define Cleft lip and cleft palate.Explain the its complications,

Surgical management and Pre and post-operative nursing management Cleft lip and cleft palate.

= Introduction

Cleft lip and cleft palate are congenital malformations resulting from the failure of fusion of maxillary processes during intrauterine development. The defect may occur either alone or together.

Definition

Cleft lip (cheiloschisis): A cleft lip result from failure of fusion of maxillary process with nose elevation on frontal prominence. The extent of defect varies from a notch in the lip (partial or incomplete cleft) to a large cleft reaching the floor of nose (complete cleft). Cleft lip can occur on one side (unilateral) or may be on both sides (bilateral).

Cleft Palate (Palatoschisis): Cleft palate results from failure of fusion of the hard palate with each other and with the soft palate. Cleft lip also usually occurs with cleft palate. Cleft palate may be complete (involving hard and soft palate, possibly including a gap in the palate) or incomplete (a 'hole' in the roof of the mouth, usually in soft palate).

Complications

Cleft lip and cleft palate leads to the following problems:

i. Feeding problems: Due to a separation in the lip or opening in the palate, sucking is ineffective and the food and liquids can pass from the mouth back through the nose. There may be aspiration of feeds.
ii. Respiratory infections: Aspiration of feeds may result in respiratory infections like aspiration pneumonia.
iii. . Ear infections/hearing loss: Children with cleft palate are at an increased risk of ear infections. Usually middle ear infections occur. If left untreated, may result in hearing loss
iv. Speech problems: Children with cleft lip or palate may have trouble in speaking. The voice of these children may take a nasal sound and speech may be difficult to understand.
v. Dental problems: Children with clefts are more prone to dental cavities and often have missing, extra, malformed or displaced teeth requiring orthodontic treatment.

Management

A Cleft lip may require one or two surgeries depending on the severity of defect. The initial surgery is usually performed at the age of 3 months. Common procedures for repair of cleft lip are Tennison Randall Triangular Flap (Z-plasty) and Millard's Rotational Advancement technique. Surgeons may also combine these two techniques, if needed.

A Cleft palate repair often requires multiple surgeries over the course of 18 years. The first surgical repair usually occurs when the baby is between 6-12 months. The initial surgery creates a functional palate, reduces the chance of fluid entering the middle ears and helps in proper development of teeth and facial bones. Children with a cleft palate may need a bone graft when they are about 8 years old to fill in the upper gum line so that it can support permanent teeth and stabilize upper jaw. About 20% of children with a cleft palate require further surgeries to help improve speech. Once the permanent teeth grow, braces may be put to straighten the teeth.

Nursing Management

Care of the Baby at Birth

- Cleft lip and cleft palate is detected immediately after birth, during initial neonatal assessment. Associated, congenital anomalies and life threatening complications should be identified for prompt management.
- This is a disfiguring defect so soon after birth, the baby looks unattractive. The defect evokes negative reaction and shock in parents. The nurse must explain to the parents about possibility of defect correction.
- Feeding of the infant with cleft lip and cleft palate is a problem because this defect reduces the infant's ability to suck.
- Breast feeding is possible with the use of palatal prosthesis (Palatal Obturator). If the baby is unable to suck the breast, expressed breast milk may be given using syringe with a rubber tube.
- Expressed breast milk or artificial feeding can also be given with long handled spoon or dropper or soft nipple with a large hole.
- Mother and family members should be demonstrated, the various techniques that can be used for feeding the baby at home.
- Explain to the parents about the risk of aspiration due to cleft palate. So they must be instructed to feed the baby in upright position.
- Small bolus should be given from the corner of the mouth.
- Give the baby sufficient time to swallow. Small frequent feeds should be given.
- Burp the baby in between the feeds and after feeding.
- Parents must be explained the importance of adequate nutrition for growth and development of the baby.
- The baby must be given all essential care including immunization, warmth, hygiene, prevention of infection etc.
- Explain about timely follow-up to the parents.

Care of the Baby before Surgery

Basic preoperative care is required. The baby must be prepared according to the surgeon's orders.

- Consent must be taken prior to surgery.
- All the investigation reports must be entered in patient's file.
- The baby must be kept NPO, at least 6 hours prior to surgery.

Care of the Baby after Surgery

- Immediately after the surgery, closely observe and monitor the vital signs of the baby.
- Observe for any bleeding from the site of surgery.
- Turn the baby's face to one side, for drainage of secretions and preventing aspiration.
- Most importantly the surgical site is to be protected from any injury, by taking the following measures

a. Position the baby on back or side and arm or elbow restraints are applied to prevent him/her from touching the suture site. These restraints must be periodically removed to exercise the arms.
b. An arched metallic device known as 'Logan's bow' must be placed over the upper lip and taped to the infant's cheeks to prevent tension at the suture line.

- Administer the prescribed analgesic, to minimize pain that causes the baby to cry causing tension on the suture line.
- Prevent infection at the site, by cleaning the operated area gently using aseptic techniques, after each feeding.
- Do not allow the baby to put any object in mouth, as this may injure the surgical repair.
- Provide love and affection to the baby, as this enhances the feeling of comfort and security in the baby.

Q 7. A. Define TEF.

b.

Explain the types and clinical features of TEF

c.

Explain pre and post-operative management of patient with TEF

= Define TEF ,

Esophageal atresia/tracheoesophageal fistula (EA/TEF) is a condition resulting from abnormal development before birth of the tube that carries food from the mouth to the stomach (the esophagus).

Tracheoesophageal fistula is an abnormal connection (fistula) between the esophagus and the trachea. TEF is a common congenital abnormality.

Enumerates Types of TEF with diagram .

= Classification EA with TEF can be classified as follows

a. Type-I: EA without fistula (8%). It is the second most common type. There is no connection of esophagus to trachea. The upper (proximal) segment and lower (distal) segment of esophagus are blind.

b. Type-II: EA with TEF (upper). It is rare and found in less than 1 percent of all cases. Upper segment of esophagus open into trachea by a fistula. The distal or lower segment is blind.

c. Type-III: EA with TEF (lower) (80-90%). It is the most common type. In this condition, the proximal or upper segment of the esophagus has blind end. The distal lower segment of esophagus connects into the trachea by a fistula.

d. Type - IV: EA with TEF both upper and lower segment. It is also rare (less than 1%). There is EA with fistula between both proximal and distal ends of trachea and esophagus.

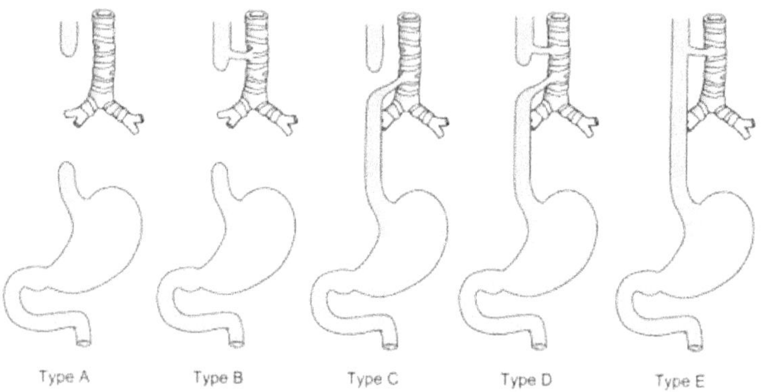

Reproduced with kind permission of John Wiley and Sons from D. M. Burge K. Shah P. Spark, et al. Contemporary management and outcomes for infants born with oesophageal atresia. BJS 2013; 100: 515–521

Types of TEF

e. Type - V: H - type TEF. It is found in about 4 percent of all cases and not usually diagnosed at birth. Both proximal / upper and distal / lower segments of esophagus open into trachea by a fistula. No EA present.

Clinical Features

The presence of maternal polyhydramnios and single umbilical artery should alert the pediatricians and pediatric nurses to look for Atresia of upper digestive tract.

The disorder is usually detected soon after birth when feeding is attempted on the basis of following manifestations:

a. Violent response occurs on feeding

   i. Infant coughs and chokes,
   ii. Fluid returns through nose and mouth
   iii. Cyanosis occur
   iv. The infant struggles

b. Excessive secretions coming out of nose and constant drooling of saliva.
c. Saliva is frothy.
d. Abdominal distension occurs in presence of type III, IV and V fistula.
e. Intermittent unexplained cyanosis and laryngospasm, caused by aspiration of accumulated saliva in blind oesophageal pouch
f. Pneumonia may occur due to overflow of milk and saliva from oesophagus through fistula into the lungs.

Management

Medical Management :

Immediate management Immediately after diagnosis, the infant should be managed with propped up position (30 ° angle) to prevent reflux of gastric secretion, and nothing per mouth, airway clearance O_2 therapy, IV fluid therapy, nasogastric tube aspiration nasogastric tube to be kept in situ and suctioning to be done frequently to prevent aspiration.

The blind pouch to be washed with normal saline to prevent blocking of tube with thick mucus.

Gastrostomy is done to decompress the stomach and to prevent aspiration and afterwards to feed the infant.

Supportive care should include maintenance of nutritional requirements and warmth, prevention of infections, antibiotics therapy, respiratory support, detection and treatment of complications, continuous monitoring of patients condition, chest physiotherapy and postural drainage.

Surgical Management

The surgical correction of defect is done by end to end anastomosis with excision of the fistula by right posterolateral thoracotomy followed by intercostal chest drainage. This is done when the infant has more than 2 kg 6 body weight and no pneumonia present and the baby is clinically stable

Surgical correction can be done in stages with division of fistula. Gastrostomy is performed in the initial stage followed by esophageal anastomosis or colonic transplant after one year.

This staging is done in small premature or very sick neonates or with other associated congenital anomalies. Other surgical interventions include cervical esophago stomy, esophago - coloplasty and esophago - gastroplasty.

Nursing Management

Nursing assessment is very important to detect the condition immediately after birth or at first feed.

Risk factors to be excluded by details history of the condition. Clinical features and problems to be assessed promptly for life - saving measures.

Nursing Management

Pre-Operative Nursing Care

1. Risk of aspiration related to structural abnormality.

- As soon as the diagnosis of TEF is made, the attempt to feed the baby is stopped.
- A nasogastric tube is put in the upper oesophageal segment and is aspirated frequently, to prevent collection and aspiration of secretions from upper oesophageal segment into the trachea (in case of type II and type IV Fistula).
- Maintain the patency of indwelling nasogastric tube, by frequently irrigating it with normal saline.
- Place the infant in semi- upright position, to prevent reflux of gastric contents into trachea (in case of Type III, IV and V Fistula).
- . Constantly observe the child for symptoms of respiratory distress like pallor, cyanosis, choking, nasal flaring etc.
- A gastrostomy tube is placed for gastric decompression, before the definitive surgery. Gastric decompression prevents reflux of gastric contents into trachea (in case of Type III and IV TEF)
- Turn the baby frequently, to prevent atelectasis and pneumonia.

- Administer the prescribed antibiotics, to prevent and treat pneumonia resulting from aspiration or reflux of gastric contents into the trachea.

2. Risk of deficient fluid volume related to inability to take oral feeds.

- As soon as the diagnosis of TEF is established, oral feedings are stopped.
- Intravenous fluids are administered, as prescribed by the physician.
- Maintain intake and output chart.
- Monitor the hydration status of the infant and look for signs of dehydration.
- A gastrostomy tube may be placed, before definitive surgery to aid in gastric decompression and provide gastrostomy feedings.

3. Impaired breathing related to frequent laryngospasm and excessive secretions in the trachea.

- In case of Type II TEF, secretions from the upper blind pouch of oesophagus may easily enter the trachea leading to laryngospasm and respiratory distress, so frequently suction the upper oesophageal segment.
- Monitor the vital signs of the infant.
- If cyanosis occurs, administer oxygen.
- Keep the infant in semi- upright position.

Post-Operative Nursing Care

1. Ineffective airway clearance related to disease process.

A cervical oesophagostomy is made to drain out secretions from upper blind oesophageal pouch, so that the secretions may not overflow and enter the trachea.

Administer oxygen to the infant.

. Ventilatory support may be provided, until the infant is clinically stable (upto 24-48 hours of surgery).

Change the infant's position frequently to prevent pooling of secretions in lungs.

2. Impaired nutrition related to surgery.

i. Feed the infant orally or by gastrostomy, depending upon the type of surgery done and infant's condition

. ii. The gastrostomy is generally attached to gravity drainage for 3 post-operative days, thereafter it is elevated and left open to allow air from the stomach to escape and gastric secretions to pass into the duodenum.

Iii. Gastrostomy feeding is started as soon as ordered.

iv. Prevent air from entering the stomach during gastrostomy feeding, as it may cause abdominal distension.

V. After 10-14 days of surgery, before starting oral feeds, an x-ray is taken, to find out whether anastomosis has healed. When healing has occurred, test feeding is given with glucose water. Slowly oral feeds are started with small amounts of clear fluids and then milk can be started.

3. Altered comfort related to chest tube drainage and surgery.

- Position the baby comfortably in semi-fowler's position.
- Administer the prescribed analgesics.
- Provide a calm and quiet environment so that the baby may rest.
- Special care should be taken that baby may not pull out the nasogastric tube, put after anastomosis of oesophageal segments. This may cause injury to the operative site. The baby's hands should be restrained.
- . Whenever possible avoid or open the restraints. Somebody should be there with the baby to hold his hands.
- Assess the type of chest drainage present. Report if saliva or blood is present in the drainage
- Keep the drainage system closed to prevent occurrence of pneumothorax.

4. Anxiety related to disease process and care of the baby after discharge.

- Discharge planning must be done.
- Explain to the parents about routine care, especially feeding the baby.
- Explain about any future surgery, if needed.
- Refer parents to genetic counselling clinic and social welfare agencies that may help them.

Q 8. HIRSCHSPRUNG'S DISEASE / MEGACOLON

= **Definition**

Hirschsprung's disease is a disorder of the gut caused due to congenital absence of ganglion cells in the submucosal and myenteric plexus of intestine . This disease is also known as Megacolon or Congenital Aganglionic Megacolon .

Pathophysiology

Hirschsprung's disease is caused by congenital absence of autonomic parasympathetic ganglion cells in the submucosal and myenteric plexus of the intestine . In majority of cases , the disorder affects the short segment of the distal colon . In 5 % cases the entire colon is affected .

Due to absence of ganglionic cells

There is lack of peristalsis in the affected portion

Functional obstruction of colon

Accumulation of gas and faeces proximal to the defect

Enlargement of the colon occurs , so it is also known as Megacolon

Clinical Features

The symptoms of congenital megacolon vary from acute obstruction in newboms to chronic constipation in older children .

In neonates and infants :

The initial symptom is failure to pass meconium .

Abdominal distension occurs within 1-2 days after birth .

Bile- stained vomiting occurs because of intestinal obstruction .

Failure to take fluids and vomiting leads to weight loss and dehydration .

Shock may develop , if condition is not treated promptly .

Episodes of diarrhea and constipation occur alternately during infancy .

Enterocolitis may occur due to faecal stagnation .

Enterocolitis may lead to dehydration and sepsis which may cause death of the infant .

In older children :

• Hirschsprung's disease is manifested by constipation with abdominal distension due to mass of faeces and gas .

When stools are passed , they foul smelling and may be expelled in pellet or ribbon like form or may be liquid in consistency .

These children are malnourished and anemic due to malabsorption of nutrients .

They have protruding abdomen and thin wasted extremities

• **Diagnostic Evaluation** :

Hirschsprung's disease suspected in a baby who has not passed meconium within 48 hours of birth , Normally , 90 % of babies pass first meconium within 24 hours and 99 % within 48 hours of birth .

On rectal examination of suspected cases , there may be an explosive leakage of gas and accumulated faeces .

On palpating the abdomen , faecal mass is felt in the left lower portion of the abdomen .

Definitive diagnosis can be made on the basis of anorectal manometry , barium enema and rectal biopsy . Rectal biopsy is the gold standard for definitive diagnosis . The biopsy shows absence of ganglion cells in the submucosa .

Management

A. Medical Management: Medical management of child having mild chronic symptoms of megacolon include :

Administration of isotonic enema

Administration of stool softeners

Low residue diet

B. Surgical Management

The aim of surgery is to remove the aganglionic bowel followed by anastomosis of the remaining portion . The surgery involves two steps . In first stage , a temporary colostomy is done above the transition zone of ganglionic and aganglionic bowel in the sigmoid or transverse colon . This enables the normal distal bowel to return to its original tone and size . Second stage involves definitive surgery , which is done when the child's weight and condition is appropriate .

Definitive surgery consists of excision of aganglionic segment with a ' pull through ' procedure enabling an anastomosis to be done between ganglionic colon and anus . The most frequently performed surgeries are those done by Swenson , Soave , Duhamel and Boley . All these procedures vary slightly from each other . After about a year of these corrective surgeries , the colostomy is closed .

Nursing Management Pre - operative Nursing Care

i . The first step , to begin the care of affected newborn is assessment . A complete history of the newborn is taken . The history shows failure to pass meconiumn and vomiting . Physical assessment of the baby shows presence of abdominal distension . In case of older children , the nurse must enquire about bowel habits of the child , including the age at which constipation started

. ii . After the diagnosis of Hirschsprung's disease , the nurse must help parents to adjust to their imperfect newborn and foster parents- Infant bonding . The nurse must explain about the disease to parents .

iii Parents are taught the procedure of giving isotonic enema , suppositories and stool softeners .

iv . A low residue diet may be given to the child , to keep the stool small in amount and soft , so that it can be evacuated easily . Soft diet including potato , rice , milk , soup , strained fruit juice , bread etc. must be given to the child .

V. Vital signs of the child are monitored to obtain baseline data about the child .

vi . Monitor abdominal girth to detect abdominal distension .

vii . Keep the child in semi - fowler's position to facilitate lung expansion and breathing .

viii . Withhold oral feeds and nasogastric aspiration is done on the night before surgery .

Repeated saline enema and bowel wash with antibiotic solution like neomycin is done in case ofolder children , to prepare the bowel for surgery .

X. Observe the child for pre - operative complications like shock , acute intestinal obstruction , bowel. perforation and dehydration .

a. The nurse observes for shock by monitoring vital signs and blood pressure .

. b . For detecting intestinal obstruction , monitor abdominal girth and observe for absence of stool , vomiting , abdominal pain and absence of bowel sounds on auscultation .

c. Perforation of intestine results in peritonitis , which is manifested by sudden relief in abdominal pain and then increased generalized pain , increased pulse rate , respiratory rate and high fever .

d . Another complication that may arise is dehydration . The nurse must assess the child properly to detect the severity of dehydration . Dehydration is indicated by reduced urine output , increased thirst , sunken eyes , poor skin turgor etc.

XI . If any of these complications arise , immediately notify the physician and provide appropriate care .

xii in the preoperative period , prepare the child for colostomy and related procedures .

Post - Operative Nursing Care Postoperative nursing care includes routine post - abdominal surgery interventions , which are as follows :

. Monitor vital signs of the child .

ii . Observe abdominal dressing or ostomy bag for bleeding .

iii . Place the child in comfortable position according to the physician's order .

iv . Monitor for abdominal distension

V. After surgery the child is NPO , so administer IV fluids as ordered . vi . Maintain fluid and electrolyte balance .

vii . Monitor for return of bowel sounds . As soon as bowel sounds return , start oral feeding .

viii . Colostomy care is to be done which includes the following :

a . Observe the stoma for its colour (normally it is pinkish or reddish- pink in colour) .

b . Observe stoma for any bleeding , purulent drainage or edema .

c . Provide bland diet to the child , which is non - irritating to stoma .

d . Apply zinc oxide ointment on skin around the stoma to prevent excoriation of skin .

e . Frequently empty the collecting bag applied on the stoma .

f . Keep the colostomy clean and dry .

g . Educate parents about colostomy care .

ix . If definitive pull - through surgery is done , following care needs to be given

a . The incision site is to be prevented from infection . There is high risk of infection from urine and stool . So , do not put diaper , in order to observe for passage of urine and stool . As soon as the baby passes urine or stool , clean and dry the child .

b . Meticulous skin care is essential .

C. IV fluids are given until peristalsis resumes , baby starts passing stool through anus and healing of the anastomosis has taken place .

d . As soon as bowel sounds return start oral feeds with glucose water and then milk .

e . Observe for indications of post- operative complications like hemorrhage , shock , abdominal distension , wound infection , peritonitis , enterocolitis etc. A serious complication of corrective surgery is leakage at the site of anastomosis leading to pelvic abscess , as evidenced by sudden abdominal distension , rise in body temperature to upto 40 ° C and extreme irritability . If any of these sign and symptom appears , notify the surgeon immediately .

X. Advice caregivers that after discharge from hospital provide adequate fluids , dietary fibre and stool softeners or bulk agents to the child in order to achieve normal bowel activity .

xi . Encouraging and supporting the family during this stressful time is the key nursing intervention .

D . DISORDERS OF CARDIOVASCULAR SYSTEM

Q 9. Define congenital heart diseases. Classify congenital heart diseases. Explain about ventricular septal defect .

= Congenital heart disease (CHD) is the structural malforma tions of the heart or great vessels, present at birth. It is the most common congenital malformations. The exact number ofprevalence is not known.

Classification

Congenital heart disease (CHD) can be grouped into three categories:

1. Acyanotic CHD: There is increased pulmonary blood flow due to left to right shunt. It includes:

Ventricular septal defect (VSD)

Atrial septal defect (ASD)

Patent ductus arteriosus (PDA)

Atrioventricular canal (AVC)

2. Cyanotic CHD: There is diminished pulmonary blood flow due to right to left shunt. It includes:

Tetralogy of Fallot (TOF) .

Tricuspid atresia (TA)

Transposition of great arteries (TGA) .

Truncus arteriosus.

Hypoplastic left heart syndrome.
Total anomalous pulmonary venous return.
Eisenmenger syndrome or complex.

3. Obstructive lesions

Coarctation of aorta
Aortic value stenosis.
Pulmonary valve stenosis.
Congenital mitral stenosis.

Ventricular Septal Defect

A ventricular septal defect (VSD) is an abnormal opening in the septum between right and left ventricles. It is the most common acyanotic congenital heart disease with left to right shunt. It is found approximately 25 percent of all CHD. The size of defect can be small or large. Large VSDs can be restrictive or nonrestrictive type. Number of defects can be single or multiple . . VSD can be found as perimembranous or muscular

- **Pathophysiology:** There is flow of oxygenated blood from high pressure left ventricle to low pressure right ventricle through the VSD. Increased right ventricular and pulmonary arterial pressure leads to pulmonary over circulation. Increased venous return to the left heart results in left heart dilation. Long standing pulmonary overcirculation causes change in pulmonary arterial bed resulting increased pulmonary -vascular resistance, which can reverse the shunt from right to left. This complicated condition is known as Eisenmenger's complex.

The child with this condition presents with cyanosis and surgical correction of VSDs is not possible in this stage. In case of a restrictive VSD (under 0.5 cm^2) higher pressure in the LV is able to cause only a limited left to right shunt. In case of nonrestrictive VSD (large, usually over 1 cm^2), magnitude of the shunt from left to right is, therefore, limited at birth due to higher pulmonary vascular resistance. In next few weeks, with the reduction in resistance, the shunt magnitude increases. VSD becomes symptomatic when the shunt magnitude becomes quite large.

Clinical manifestations:

Small VSDs are asymptomatic. In large defects, symptoms develops within one to 2 months of age. The manifestations are recurrent chest infections, feeding difficulties, tachypnea, exertional dyspnea, pale, delicate looking, tachycardia, excessive sweating associated with feeding, poor weight gain, failure to thrive, hepatomegaly, biventricular hypertrophy and CCF.

The characteristic loud pansystolic murmur heard maximal down the left sternal border, usually accompanied by the thrill. The functional diastolic murmur may present.

Diagnostic evaluation: History of illness, physical exami nation and auscultation of harsh systolic murmur and pulmonary second sound (p_2) are important for diagnosis of the condition. Chest X-ray shows enlargement of the heart and increased pulmonary vascular marking. ECG reveals biventricular hypertrophy. Two-dimensional echocardiogram with Doppler study and color flow mapping are performed to identify the size, number, site of defect and associated problems.

Management: In small VSD, usually no medical management is required. Surgical repair may be indicated in some cases. Prevention of complications is very essential measures. Spontaneous closure of VSD occurs in 30 to 50 percent cases with small defects. In large VSD, initial management of associated problems like CCF and endocarditis, should be done with appropriate treatment. Early surgical repair is planned after management of complications.

Surgery is done as one-stage or two-stage operation. One stage operation with patch closure of VSD by open-heart method can be performed. Two-stage approach is done with first stage, to band the pulmonary artery to restrict pulmonary blood flow by closed-heart method. Second stage operation is done to patch close the VSD and remove the PA band. Surgery is contraindicated in shunt reversal. Long-term prognosis after corrective surgery is excellent. Expert nursing management is important during surgical interventions and in complications. Long-term follow-up and monitoring of ventricular functions are important measures to promote excellent prognosis.

Complications: The common complications of VSD are CCF, recurrent respiratory tract infections, infective endo carditis, Eisenmenger's syndrome, pulmonary stenosis, pulmonary hypertension and failure to thrive. Postoperative complications after thoracic surgery may be life-threatening for the child.

Q10 .Explain the causative predisposing factors for acute rheumatic fever.

= Rheumatic fever is an immunological disorder initiated by group A beta hemolytic streptococcus.

It is a systemic inflammatory disease of childhood that can involve the heart , joints, central nervous system, skin and connective tissues .

Risk factors

Things that may increase the risk of rheumatic fever include:

- **Genes.** Some people have one or more genes that might make them more likely to develop rheumatic fever.
- **Specific type of strep bacteria.** Certain strains of strep bacteria are more likely to contribute to rheumatic fever than are other strains.
- **Environmental factors.** A greater risk of rheumatic fever is associated with overcrowding, poor sanitation and other conditions that can cause strep bacteria to easily spread among many people.
- Rheumatic fever is caused by a bacterium called group A *Streptococcus*. This bacterium causes strep throat or, in a small percentage of people, scarlet fever. It's an inflammatory disorder.
- Rheumatic fever causes the body to attack its own tissues. This reaction causes widespread inflammation throughout the body, which is the basis for all symptoms of rheumatic fever.

Q11. Jones criteria for Rheumatic fever

= Rheumatic fever is an immunological disorder initiated by group A beta hemolytic streptococcus.

It is a systemic inflammatory disease of childhood that can involve the heart , joints, central nervous system, skin and connective tissues .

The diagnosis of ARF can be made by applying the modified (1992) Jones criteria. Diagnosis requires evidence of recent streptococcal infection and 2 major criteria, or 1 major and 2 minor criteria.

Major Criteria

Polyarthritis: Migrating arthritis that typically affects the knees, ankles, elbows and wrists. The joints are very painful and symptoms are very responsive to anti inflammatory medicines.

Carditis: All layers of cardiac tissue are affected (pericardium, epicardium, myocardium, endocardium). The patient may have a new or changing murmur, with mitral regurgitation being the most common followed by aortic insufficiency.

Chorea: Also known as Syndenham's chorea, or "St. Vitus' dance." Chorea consists of abrupt, purposeless, jerky, uncoordinated movements, especially affecting the hands, feet, tongue and face. This may be the ONLY manifestation of ARF.

Erythema marginatum: A non-pruritic rash that com monly affects the trunk and proximal extremities, but spares the face. The rash typically migrates from cen tral areas to periphery, forming a snakelike ring while clear ing in the middle and has well - defined borders. This rash is made worse with heat.

Subcutaneous nodules (a form of Aschoff bodies): Small non-tender, firm collections of collagen fibers on the back of the wrist, the outside elbow, and the front of the knees. These now occur infrequently.

An additional way **to remember the major criteria** is by the mnemonic:

CANCER

C: Carditis

A: Arthritis

N: Nodules (subcutaneous)

C: Chorea

ER: Erythema Marginatum

Minor Criteria

Arthralgia: Pain on joint movement without evidence of swelling or heat

Fever

Previous ARF or rheumatic heart disease

Leukocytosis, elevated ESR and CRP

Prolonged P - R interval on ECG

Management

Bedrest is important in the management of children with rheumatic fever. It is needed for at least 6 to 8 weeks till the rheumatic activity is disappeared.

Nutritious diet to be provided with sufficient amount of protein, vitamins and micronutrients. Salt restriction is not necessary unless CCF is present. Avoid rich spicy food.

Antibiotic therapy, penicillin is administered after skin test to eradicate streptococcal infection. Initially, procaine penicillin 4 lacks units deep IM, twice a day is given for 10 to 14 days. Then the long-acting benzathine penicillin 1.2 mega units every 21 days or 0.6 mega unit every 15 days to be given. Oral penicillin 4 lakhs units (250 mg), every 4 to 6 hours for 10 to 14 days can be also given. Erythromycin can be used in penicillin sensitive patients.

Aspirin is administered as suppressive therapy to control pain and inflammation of joints. The dose of aspirin is 90 to 120 mg/kg/ day in 4 divided doses. It may be needed for 12 weeks. The dose can be modified for the individual patients. Aspirin should not be given in empty stomach. Antacid to be given just prior to or with the aspirin.

Steroid (prednisolone) therapy is given as suppressive therapy along with aspirin. The initial dose is 40 to 60 mg/ day or 2 mg/kg/

day in 4 divided doses, for 7 to 10 days. Then the dose is reduced to 1 mg/kg/day. It should be tapered off gradually over 12 weeks period and used for patients having carditis with or without CCF.

Management of chorea can be done with diazepam or phenobarbitone.

Treatment of complications, if present, especially for CCF should be done. Symptomatic care to be provided accordingly.

Nursing Management

Nursing assessment is vital for the care of the child with rheumatic fever. It should include special attention to vital signs, cardiac monitoring (ECG, heart sound), pain assessment and other associated problems.

Important nursing diagnoses are (a) decreased cardiac output related to carditis (b) pain related to polyarthritis (e) risk of injury related to involuntary movements in chorea, (d) anxiety related to disease process, (e) knowledge deficit related to long-term treatment and prognosis of the acquired heart disease.

Nursing Interventions

Nursing interventions should emphasize on the followings along with routine care:

Improving cardiac output by:

- Providing rest as long as rheumatic activity and heart failure persist. In milder cases light indoor activity is allowed.
- Organizing nursing care with uninterrupted rest and modifying activities.
- maintaining normal body temperature by managing fever.
- Providing bland diet with adequate nutrition and fluid intake with salt restriction in case of CCF.
- Administering medication as prescribed with necessary precautions.
- Monitoring cardiac functions, intake-output and features of improvement or deterioration.

Relieving pain by:

- Administering anti-inflammatory analgesics as prescribed and assessing features of aspirin toxicity.
- Providing comfortable position and support to the inflamed joints.
- Arranging diversional activities and play materials according to age and choice of the child.

Protecting the child from injury by:

- Removing hard and sharp objects from the child's reach.
- Assisting the child in feeding, ambulation and other fine motor activities and channelization of the stress.
- Administration of drugs to control the chorea.
- Explaining about self-limiting course of the condition and importance about physical and mental rest.
- hlealth teaching for maintenance of health and prevention of Complications:
- Explaining the duration of treatment, its importance and compliance, activity restriction, follow-up, continuationof school performance and improvement of living standard.
- Instructing about preventive measures.

E . DISORDERS OF HEMATOLOGICAL SYSTEMS.

Q .12. Define anemia , Enumerate the causes of the anemia , enumerate the nursing management of anemia.

=Anemia is the most common blood disorder in infant and children, especially of poor socioeconomic group. Anemia is defined as the reduction in the number and quality of circulating red blood cells when the hemoglobin content is below the normal level for particular age, resulting in decreased oxygen carrying capacity.

World Health Organization (WHO) proposed the cut-off points of Hb level for different age groups for the diagnosis of

a. Children 6 months to 6 years-11 g/dL

b. Children 6 years to 14 years-12 g/dL

c Above 14 years-

Male-13 g/dL –

Female-12 g/dL

Mild anemia (10.0-10.9 g/dL)-26.3 percent

Moderate anemia (7.0-9.9 g/dL)-40.2 percent

Severe anemia (less than 7 g/dL)-2.9 percent

Any anemia (Hb level less than 11 g/dL) is found in 69.5 percent children.

Causes of Anemia

Red blood cells (RBCs) and hemoglobin are normally formed and destroyed at the same rate. But when formation of RBC and hemoglobin is decreased and their destruction is increased then anemia develops. The oxygen carrying capacity and CO., removing capacity are decreased. There are various causes of anemia but in some cases causes can beidiopathic.

Impaired ofRBC production: Impaired of RBC production due to deficiency of hemopoietic factors in nutritional deficiency (nutritional anemia)

The most common nutritional anemiais iron deficiency anemia. Other nutritional deficiency conditions causing anemia are folic acid deficiency, vitamin B, 2 deficiency, vitamin B deficiency and vitamin C deficiency.

Increased destruction of RBCs (hemolytic anemia)

1. Hemolysis due to intrinsic factors

. **i. Abnormal hemoglobin synthesis**-thalassemia, sickle cell disease **Causes of anemia can be described as follows:**

ii. Enzymatic defect-Glucose-6-phosphate-dehy drogenase deficiency.

iii. Abnormalities in RBC membrane or structural defects of RBC-Hereditary spherocytosis.

2. Hemolysis due to extrinsic factors

i. Infections-malaria, kala-azar.

ii. Antibody reaction-Rh or ABO isoimmunization, autoimmune hemolytic anemia, lupus.

iii. Drugs-Primaquine, phenacetin, phenytoin. iv. Poisoning-Lead. v. Burns

vi. Splenomegaly.

C. Increased blood loss:

1. Acute-Trauma, epistaxis, bleeding diathesis (leukemia, purpura, hemophilia), hemorrhagic disease of newborn and scurvy. blood loss (hemorrhagic anemia)

2. Chronic-Hookworms, bleeding piles, chronic dysentery, esophageal varices.

d. Decreased RBC production (bone marrow depression)

1. Primary-Hypoplasia or aplasia, Fanconi anemia.

2. Secondary-Irradiation, infections, chronic illness like nephritis, leukemia and other neoplastic diseases, tuberculosis, liver disease, hypothyroidism and drug therapy (chloramphenicol, sulfas)

Clinical Manifestations

The early symptoms of anemia are fatique, listlessness and anorexia. Late symptoms may include pallor (skin, nail bed, mucous membrane), weakness, vertigo, headache, malaise and drowsiness.

Other features are sore tongue, gastro intestinal problems, tachypnea, shortness of breath on exertion, tachycardia, palpitations, etc. Jaundice, petechiae and ecchymosis may present in some cases.

Hepatomegaly may be associated feature in hemoglobinopathies and liver disorders. Enlarged lymph gland may be found in leukemia, infections, malignancy and myeloproliferative disorders.

Management

Medical management of anemia depends upon the specific cause of the condition.

Anemia due to excessive blood loss should be treated accordingly. Acute blood loss needs immediate control of bleeding and to restore blood volume by IV infusion, blood transfusion along with treatment of shock and the cause of bleeding.

Chronic blood loss usually produces iron deficiency anemia. The exact cause should be detected and treatment should be planned according to the specific cause.

Anemia due to excessive blood cell destruction requires the identification and treatment of specific hemolytic disorder.

Anemia due to decreased blood cell formation is mainly due to deficiency states and bone marrow disorders. Specific deficiency of iron, folic acid, vitamin B_1 2, etc should be detected and treatment to be done with replacement therapy of specific nutrients. In case of bone marrow depressions, the specific cause (like drugs, toxins) to be identified and treatment to be performed by removal of offending agents.

Nursing Management

Nursing assessment is the corner stone of nursing inter ventions. It is done by obtaining details history to detect poten tial causes of the condition. History of present complaints, past illness, chronic diseases, presence of infections, worm infestations, exposure to medications, poisons, dietary habits, behavioral problems like pica and history of familial diseases are important aspects of assessment.

Physical examination to be done to exclude the presence of clinical features like pallor of skin and mucous membrane with other signs and symptoms related to anemia. Assessment of anthropometric data (height, weight, MUAC, skin fold thickness, head and chest circumference), vital signs and review of laboratory investigations are important to identify the problems and to implement the care

Q 13. Define thalessemia , Explain the clinical manifestation and Mediacal management of the Thalessemia . Nursing diagnosis with interventions .

= Thalassemia is a group of hereditary hemolytic anemia characterized by reduction in the synthesis of hemoglobin.

It produces hypochromic microcytic anemia due to defective hemoglobinization of RBCs, hemolysis and ineffective erythropoiesis. Thalassemia can be considered as hemoly tic and hypoproliferative anemia related to abnormal hemoglobin.

Clinical Manifestations of Thalassemia

Thalassemia r usually manifested at the age of 3 months with progressive pallor, jaundice, hepatosplenomegaly, recurrent respiratory infections, enlargement of lymph nodes and growth failure.

In severe cases facial appearance becomes mongoloid and characterized by bossing of the skull, prominent frontal and parietal eminences with flat vault and straight forehead.

Maxilla becomes prominent with exposure of malformed teeth. Bridge of the nose becomes depressed with puffy eyes.

Anorexia, poor feeding and abdominal distension may present. Irregular fever may occur due to intercurrent infections, and increased metabolic activity.

Increased pigmentation of the skin found as bronze discoloration due to high level of melanin and hemosiderin.

Hypogonadism, poor nutritional status with reduced activity level are common findings. Marked growth retardation is observed. Skeletal changes are marked and pathological fracture may occur due to osteoporosis.

Management

Repeated Blood Transfusion

It is given at regular interval to maintain the hemoglobin level at least 10 to 11 g/dL. Interval and amount of blood transfusion depends upon the level of hemoglobin of the child. Usually 10 to 15 mL/kg every 2 to 3 weeks washed packed RBCs are transfused. Special precautions to be taken duringtransfusion to prevent complications.

Iron Chelation Therapy

Iron chelating agent desferrioxamine (Desferal) is recom mended to prevent complications of repeated blood transfusions, i.e. hemosiderosis and hemochromatosis. It is given as continuous subcutaneous infusion in the dose of 25 to 50 mg/kg/day over a period of 8 hours to 12 hours.

Splenectomy

Splenectomy is indicated when the child need very frequent blood transfusion and develop hypersplenism or big spleen causing discomfort.

Folic Acid Supplementations

Folic acid supplementations are recommended whereas iron therapy and dietary iron should be avoided to prevent more iron deposition.

Supportive Management

Supportive management is important to manage associated problems and to treat complications (like CCF, hepatic failure). Vaccination with hepatitis 'B' to be given to prevent transfusion related infection along with other routine immunization. Emotional support is very essential to the parents and child. Basic supportive nursing care are very important to prevent various complications.

Bone Marrow Transplantation

Bone marrow transplantation is an effective treatment mod ality with potential of curing thalassemia. Defective stem cells are replaced by normal stem cells. It is extremely expensive and possible in only very selective cases.

New Approaches

New approaches in the management of thalassemia are gene therapy and gene manipulation. In gene therapy, insertion of normal gene is done in the stem cells to correct underlying defect. Itis done in two approaches, i.e. somatic and transgenic. In gene manipulation, excess of alpha chains is decreased by increasing the gamma chains.

Nursing Management

Nursing assessment should be done based on subjective and objective data to formulate the nursing diagnoses for the particular child and to implement the nursing interventions.

The important nursing diagnoses for a thalassemic child are as follows:

1. Altered tissue perfusion related to abnormal hemoglobin.
2. Risk of infection related to anemia.
3. Activity intolerance related to anemia, CCF, etc.
4. Chronic pain related to skeletal changes.
5. Body image disturbances related the bony changes and facial deformities.
6. Ineffective family coping related to poor prognosis.
7. Knowledge deficit related to child care in long-term chronic illness with hemolytic anemia.

Nursing Interventions

- Nursing interventions should emphasized on the following aspects:
- Assessment of child condition to prevent complications that can be done as hospital based or community based home).
- Preparation for repeated hospitalization for treatment of the disease and its complications based . (at home)
- Arrangement of necessary diagnostic measures.
- Administration of blood transfusion and iron chelating agent with appropriate precautions for specific therapy.
- Provision of supportive care with rest, comfort, nutritious diet with restriction of iron containing food. Vitamin supplementation, immunization, hygienic care and other symptomatic care.
- Prevention of infection by aseptic techniques and promotion of general cleanliness.
- Preoperative and postoperative care during splenectomy with necessary health education after the surgery.
- Information regarding treatment plan, prognosis and complications to be given to parent and family members with appropriate explanation.
- Emotional support to the parents and family for effective coping about the stress of the illness.

- Teaching the parent about importance of follow-up, blood transfusion, investigations, signs of complications, dietary restriction, activity modification, recreation, diversion and available treatment facilities.
- Referral and necessary guidance for available support services and community facilities.

Q 14. Define leukemia , Describe the Clinical Manifestations, Pathophysiology , Mediacal and Nursing management of leukemia.

= Leukemia is the most common type of childhood malignancy characterized by persistent and uncontrolled production of immature and abnormal white blood cells.

It is a disease of abnormal proliferation and maturation of bone marrow which interferes with the production of normal RBCs, WBCs and platelets.

Clinical Manifestations

Clinical presentations of leukemia depend upon types of leukemic cells. The onset is usually acute or insidious.

The ALL is a great imitator with vague and varied signs and symptoms, resembling almost any disease.

The initial manifestations are fever anorexia, malaise, weakness, petechiae, purpura, ecchymosis and bleeding. The child may present with progressive pallor, decreased activity level, weight loss and muscle wasting.

The child may complain abdominal pain, bone pain, joint pain and sternal tenderness. Hepatosplenomegaly, hematemesis, melena, hematuria, oral infections are common associated features.

Excessive bleeding from nose prick or minor injury or minor operation like tooth extraction may be the first alarming features.

Rarely lymphadenopathy may found in T-cell ALL or leukemic transformation of lymphoma.

Central nervous system (CNS) involvement or meningeal leukemia may be manifested with headache, vomiting, drowsiness, unconsciousness, convulsions, cranial nerve involvement, papilledema, blurred or double vision.

Management ;

The effective treatment is available for the leukemia. It includes chemotherapy, radiation therapy, and bone marrow transplantation.

Nursing Management of a Child with Leukemia

Nursing assessment should be done on the basis of subjective and objective data. The important nursing diagnoses are:

a. Anxiety of the parent related to diagnosis of malignant disease.

b. Risk for infections and bleeding related to abnormal bone marrow functions.

C. Pain related to infiltration of leukemic cells.

d. Activity intolerance related to fatigue resulting from disease process.

e. Alternation of body temperature, more than normal due to infections.

f. Altered nutrition, less than body requirement related to anorexia, nausea and gingival ulcers.

Nursing Interventions

a. Providing emotional support to the parent to reduce parental anxiety. Encouraging the parents to express their feeling and answering their questions honestly. Necessary informations and instructions to be given to the parents and family members to avail support services, community resources and religious help to adjust with the stress situation.

b. Preventing infections and hemorrhage. The following measures to be followed:

- Maintaining aseptic technique, hygienic measures, general cleanliness, good handwashing practices, restriction of visitors and taking precautions during any invasive procedures.

- Administering antibiotics, as prescribed. Oral and IV route to be used. Intramuscular injection should be best avoided.
- Precautions to be taken during blood transfusion.
- Avoiding injury. Soft toothbrush can be used for dental care. Soft jelly to be applied for dry lips. Non irritating mouth wash to be used, no alcohol or H_2O_2 to be used. Breaking of skin and mucous membrane to be avoided.
- Monitoring vital signs, urinary output, hydration level, signs of infections, bleeding or any other complications.

c. Relieving pain by rest, comfort, minimizing exertion, promoting relaxation and diversion and administering prescribed analgesics.

d. Assisting in activity of daily living (ADL), promoting hygienic care and minimizing disturbance during nursing interventions by gentle approach.

e. Maintaining normal body temperature by tepid sponge in high fever, airy environment, adequate fluid intake, avoiding overclothing and hot environment, administering antipyretics and other prescribed drugs. Recording vital signs 4 hourly. Avoiding use of rectal thermometer.

f. Promoting adequate nutritional intake with high nutritious diet with small frequent feed. Avoiding high salty food, when steroids are given. Antiemetics to be given to prevent vomiting. Diet should be attractive and tasty to promote intake of more amount.

g. Explaining about the change of body image, especially in case of alopecia due to chemotherapy. Ensuring about future change and contacting with people having new hair following alopecia.

h. Reducing fear of the children by allowing parent with them during procedures, improving IPR and allowing play materials.

i. Teaching the parents about health maintenance regarding regular blood testing, chemotherapy or other mode of management, possible complications and their warning signs, necessary medical help and follow-up.

F . DISORDERS OF KIDNEY AND URINARY TRACK.

Q 15. Epispadias

= Epispadias is the congenital abnormal urethral opening on the dorsal aspect of the penis. Urethra is displaced dorsally due to abnormal development of the infraumbilical wall and upper wall of the urethra. It is usually associated with exstrophy of bladder and ambiguous genitalia.

Rarely it may found in female infants.

Classification

Epispadias in male child can be classified as:

Anterior epispadias with normal continence.

Glandular

Balanitic or penile.

Posterior epispadias-associated bladder neck and incontinence of urine

Penopubic

Subsymphyseal

The male infants with epispadias are having short and broad penis with dorsal curvature.

In females, a cleft extends along the roof or entire urethra, involving the bladder neck.

Urethra is short and patulous.

Female epispadias can be classified as:

Bifid clitoris with no incontinence of urine. Subsymphyseal with incontinence of urine.

In both male and female, pubic bones are usually found separated, along with epispadias.

Management

Management of epispadias is done by the surgical correction usually in three stages. First stage operation is done in about 1.5 to 2 years of age for penile lengthening, elongation of urethral strip and chordee correction. Second stage opera tion is done at least 6 months after first stage for urethral reconstruction.

Third stage operation is done about 3 to 4 years of age for bladder neck reconstruction and correction of VUR. Cystoplasty can be done to enhance the bladder capacity after 2 to 3 years of 3rd stage operation.

Supportive nursing care should emphasize on prevention of infections, emotional support for long-term management schedule and routine preoperative and postoperative management.

Health maintenance and promotion of growth and development should be emphasized by balanced diet, immunization, hygienic measures and parental guidance.

Q 16. Hypospadias

= Hypospadias is the congenital abnormal urethral opening on the ventral aspect (under surface) of the penis.

It is one of the commonest malformations of male children. Undescended testes or inguinal hernia or upper urinary tract anomalies may be associated with hypospadias

. It may found in females as urethral opening in the vagina with dribbling of urine.

Classification

Hypospadias can be classified depending upon the site of the urethral meatus. .

Anterior hypospadias (65-70%): It may be found as glandular or coronal or on distal penile shaft.

Middle (10-15%) penile shaft hypospadias.

Posterior hypospadias (20%): It may be found on proximal penile shaft or as penoscrotal, scrotal or perineal type.

Problems Related to Hypospadias

A child with hypospadias may have following problems:

Presence of painful downward curvature of the penis during erection as chordee.

Due to chordee, there is deflected stream of urine and the child wets his thigh during urination.

Inability to void urine while standing, in case of penoscrotal, scrotal and perineal hypospadias. It also may found with the penis in the normal elevated position.

If appropriate management is not done or left untreated, the condition, in later life, interferes during sexual intercourse with difficulty in penetration due to the presence of chordee. Severe forms of hypospadias interferes with reproductive ability as the sperms are deposited outside the vagina due to proximal situation of meatus.

There can be meatal stenosis, fistula, urethral stricture or stenosis or diverticulum.

Management

Management of hypospadias is done by surgical reconstruc tion to obtain straight penis at erection, to form urethral tube and urethral meatus at the tip of glans penis. Meatotomy is done at any age after birth.

Chordee correction and advancement of prepuce can be done at the age of 2 to 3 years.

Urethroplasty is done 3 to 4 months after chordee correction. The surgical repair should be completed before admission to the school. Operation can be performed as multistage or single stage repair.

Q 17. WILMS'TUMOR (NEPHROBLASTOMA)

Max Wilms, German surgeon described this most common renal tumor of childhood. It is associated with chromosomes deletions, especially from chromosomes11 and 16.

Wilms' tumor is a rapidly developing highly malignant embryonal tumor usually diagnosed within 3 years of age. It is generally unilateral and can be familial in some cases. It may be associated with other congenital anomalies, like hemihypertrophy of the vertebrae, genitourinary anomalies, aniridia, ambiguous genitalia, etc.

This tumor develops within the kidney parenchyma, distorting it and invading the surrounding tissues. The tumor tends to grow in a concentric fashion invading the adjacent renal parenchyma.

Characteristically a well developed capsule is present. Hemorrhage, necrosis and calcification may occur rarely. Metastatic spread occurs by lymphatics to the renal hilar, periaortic and pericaval lymph nodes.

Distant blood borne metastasis occurs most frequently in the lungs, bone and liver.

Clinical Manifestations

Majority ofthe affected children present with an asymptomatic abdominal mass, detected during routine examination or by the mother during daily bath or undressing the child. Increasing abdominal girth is important finding.

Microscopic hematuria, pain abdomen, fever, pallor, hypertension and superficial venous engorgement may present. Gross hematuria indicates advanced Stage III or Stage IV tumor. On examination large, smooth, fixed, firmed, nontender palpable mass detected in the flank.

Clinical Features

Wilm's tumor is asymptomatic in early stages:

The most common presenting feature of Wilm's tumor is presence of an abdominal mass or an enlarging abdomen.

The mass is discovered accidently by parents during diaper changing or bathing the baby or may be detected when the child complains of abdominal discomfort.

Other features include Pain, if tumor is rapidly enlarging or due to hemorrhage, necrosis or invasion of neighbouring structures.

Urethral obstruction, if the tumor is large, which may lead to urinary infection.

Anorexia

Hematuria High blood pressure Increased growth on only one side of body

Nausea and vomiting

Clinical Staging of Wilms' Tumor

This staging helps to determine prognosis and survival of the patients.

- Stage I: Tumor limited to kidney and can be fully excised. Renal capsule is intact. Tumor not ruptured and no residual tumor after excision.
- Stage II: Tumor extend beyond kidney but can be completely excised. There is regional extension of the tumor by penetration through renal capsule. Vessels outside kidney are either infiltrated or contain tumor thrombus. No residual tumor is apparent beyond the margins of resection.
- Stage III: Residual nonhematogenous extension of the tumor confined to the abdomen following surgery. Involvement of hilar, periaortic or other lymph nodes may present. The tumor cannot be completely resectable because of local infiltration into the vital structure.
- Stage IV: Hematogenous metastasis to distant organs, i.e. lungs, liver, brain, etc.
- Stage V: Bilateral renal involvement which occurs in 5 to 8 percent of the cases.

Management

Management of Wilm's tumor depends upon histological findings, clinical staging and metastasis.

Stage I and II Wilm's tumors with favorable histology are usually managed with nephrectomy and chemotherapy for 18 weeks.

Stage III, IV and V tumors are treated with nephrectomy, abdominal radiotherapy and chemotherapy for 24 weeks. Preoperative radiotherapy and chemotherapy are indicated in massive tumors.

Chemotherapy is usually administered with vincristine, dactinomycin, actinomycin, adriamycin, doxorubicin and cyclophosphamide.

Radio therapy is not given in children below one year of age. Nursing management should include special care during nephrectomy, radiotherapy and chemotherapy.

Reducing anxiety of the parents, by explanation, involvement in child care and teaching long-term home-based care are important nursing interventions to help the family to cope with the situation.

Q 18.Define nephrotic syndrome , Explain the Causes, pathophysiology of nephritic syndrome, Exaplain the nursing management .

= **Introduction**

The nephrotic syndrome is a clinical state characterized by proteinuria, hypoalbuminemia, hyperlipidemia and edema, sometimes accompanied by hematuria, hypertension and reduced glomerular filteration rate.

Definition

Nephrotic syndrome is clinical manifestation of a large number of glomerular disorders. It is characterized by massive proteinuria, hypoalbuminemia, hyperlipidemia and edema which is generalized and also known as anasarca or dropsy.

Primary causes of nephrotic syndrome are usually described by the histology. i.e. minimal change disease (MCD) like minimal change nephropathy which is the most common cause of nephrotic syndrome in children, and focal segmental glomerulosclerosis which is the most common cause of nephrotic syndrome in adults. When it is due systemic disease, it is termed as secondary nephrotic syndrome.

Causes

1. Primary renal causes: Minimal change nephropathy
Glomerulosclerosis
Acute post streptoccal glomerulonephritis
Immune complex glomerulonephritis
2. Systemic causes
● Infections • Toxins- Mercury, Bismuth,
Gold Allergies- Bee sting, Serum sickness,
Inhaled pollen, Food allergy.

Cardiovascular-Sickle cell disease, Renal vein thrombosis, Congestive Heart Failure

Malignancies- Leukemia

Others-Amyloidosis, Systemic Lupus Erythematous, Anaphylactic purpura

Pathophysiology

Due to any pathological condition, there is alteration in glomerular basement membrane which increases the glomerular permeability to plasma proteins. Proteinuria occurs and plasma proteins decrease. The colloidal osmotic pressure which holds water in blood vessels is decreased due to decreased amount of serum albumin. This allows fluids to flow from capillaries into the tissues. Thus vascular volume decreases which stimulates the secretion of aldosterone from adrenals thereby leading to retention of sodium and water, leading to increasing edema.

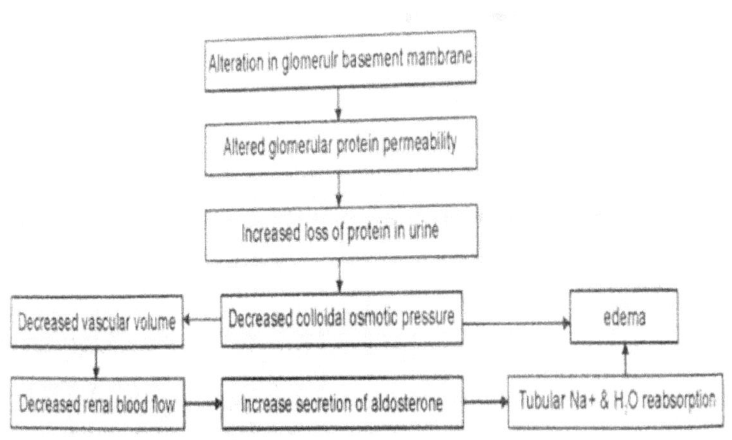

Fig. 4: Pathophysiology of Nephrotic Syndrome

pathophysiology of nephritic syndrome,

Clinical Manifestations

The onset is slow. Features of nephrotic syndrome include:

- Edema around eyes, legs and labia
- Anasarca (generalized body edema)
- Ascites
- Hydrothorax and hydrocele
- Decrease urine output, urine appears to be frothy, and has increased specific gravity
- Hematuria
- Fever, rash and joint pain
- Pallor
- Irritabiltiy
- Loss of appetite but weight gain
- Susceptibility to infections.

Nursing Management

Care during Hospitalization

Child is hospitalized for initial therapy. Parents may not understand importance of hospitalization because initially the child is symptomless. During hospitalization parents should be involved in child care and goal setting.

Nurses should regularly monitor the vital signs and check the child's daily weight.

Monitor signs of infection and edema.

Detailed charting of intake/output must be done to monitor child's response to medical therapy.

Daily urine examination for albumin is required.

Administer the prescribed Medications

Children with nephrotic syndrome are receiving steroids so the nurse must be aware of the side effects of these drugs.

Patients should be observed for gastrointestinal bleeding, gastrointestinal ulcers, hyperglycemia and cataract.

Steroid is continued till the child is protein-free, thereafter the drug dose is decreased gradually.

Maintain fluid and electrolyte balance

Nurse should monitor serum sodium level of the child. Fluid intake either Oral/IV should be strictly monitored. Child is assessed for venous stasis, ascites and pulmonary edema.

Prevention of infection

The child is on corticosteroid therapy (immunosuppressant) and there is loss of immunoglobulin in urine, so these children are at greater risk of infection. Strict aseptic techniques should be used during invasive procedures. Monitor vital signs to detect earty signs of infection,

Promote Rest

Provide passive play to the child as tolerated. E.g. watching T.V. reading story books etc. Allow a period of rest after activities. Limit visitors during acute phase of illness.

Provide Emotional Support

Explain parents about the disease and its treatment. Allow the parents and child to express their feelings. Due to sudden weight gain and disturbed body image, child may manifest with behavioral changes, may refuse to look at mirror and has decreased interest in appearance. Enhance the body image of the child. Encourage child to wear own clothes rather than hospital clothes as this makes the child feel good.

Discharge Planning and Home care teaching:

Explain to parents about treatment programme, follow up and risk of relapse.

Q 00 A. Define Acute glomerulonephritis.

B. explain the Pathophysiology, clinical features of acute glomerulonephritis

C. complications and nursing care plan of acute glomerulonephritis

= Definition

Acute glomerulonephritis is an acute or sudden inflammation of glomeruli within the kidneys. This inflammation results in acute renal failure.

Etiology

The etiologic agent is usually a bacteria or virus. The most common organism is Beta Hemolytic streptococcus. The primary site or infection is usually the throat or the skin, after which nephritis occurs.

Pathophysiology

Pathophysiology

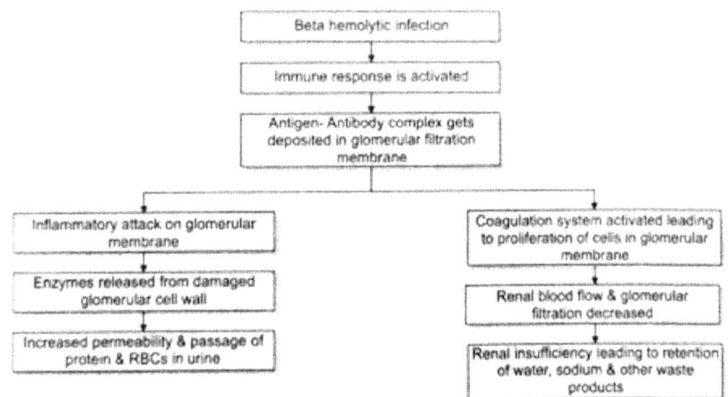

Fig. 3: Pathophysiology of glomerulonephritis

Pathophysiology

On infection with Beta hemolytic streptococcus, it invades the child's system. The immune system responds by producing antibodies which fight the infectious agents or antigens. The antigen and antibody complex forms, which gets deposited in the renal glomeruli. This leads to inflammation of glours leading to edema and hypertension.

Clinical Features

The onset of glomerulonephritis is sudden or acute.

The clinical features are as

- Hematuria
- Oliguria Tea-coloured urine due to hematuria
- Periorbital oedema
- Anasarca .

- Hypertension (very common and occurs in over half of the patients)
- A minal pain
- Fever
- Fatigue and lethargy

Management

The aims of management are:

To identify and treat the source of infection.

To maintain fluid and electrolyte balance.

To maintain blood pressure within normal range.

For the achievement of these aims, following needs to be done:

1. A detailed history and thorough physical examination is essential to find out the primary site of infection.

ii. Children with normal blood pressure and urine output can be managed at home with the administration of prescribed antibiotics.

iii. Children with generalized edema, hematuria and hypertension need to be hospitalized because of the probability of developing acute renal failure. The child should be given complete rest during acute phase.

iv. Hypertension needs to be treated with antihypertensive like Hydralazine and Methyldopa.

V. Generalized edema requires administration of diuretics like Frusemide (Lasix) in a dose of 1-3 mg/kg/dose orally (2-3 times a day) or intravenously, repeated after every 2-6 hours.

vi. Sodium, Potassium and fluid in take may be restricted to treat mild hypertension.

vii. A course of antibiotics is administered to eradicate the infectious agent.

viii. In presence of severe azotemia, protein intake may also be restricted.

Nursing Management

i. History taking and assessment

The nurse must obtain complete history of past illnesses and infections. Assess the child's weight, urine output and look for the presence of manifestations of glomerulonephritis.

ii. Monitor fluid status

Monitor fluid and electrolyte status of the child, by assessing daily body weight, periorbital edema and intake and output.

Monitor the vital signs of the child.

Monitor the degree of ascites, by measuring abdominal girth daily.

- Monitor blood pressure and administer the prescribed antihypertensives.
- Restrict fluid, salt and potassium intake, if prescribed.

iii. Prevent from infection Impaired renal function places the child at risk for infection so:

Monitor the child for signs of infection like fever, malaise and elevated WBCs.

- Educate the parents regarding good hand washing technique.

Limit the number of visitors.

Nobody with upper respiratory infection should attend the child, as the child is already infected.

iv. Prevent skin breakdown

As the child may have generalized edema, there are chances of skin breakdown, so:

Turn the child frequently and keep changing his position.

Keep the child clean and dry.

Keep the bed sheet tight and wrinkle free.

Provide frequent back care and skin care.

V. Meet the nutritional needs of the child

Anorexia during acute phase is the greatest challenge in meeting the nutritional needs of the child.

Provide low protein and no added salt diet to the child.

Provide food according to the likes and dislikes of the child.

Allow the child to eat with other children, as this may motivate him to eat.

vi. Emotional support

The parents may blame themselves for the child's condition. So discuss with them the causes and treatment and correct their misconceptions.

Provide emotional support to the parents.

Answer the queries of the parents and help them to ventilate their feelings.

G . DISORDER OF NEUROLOGICAL SYSTEM

Q19. Define Meningitis , Enlist the clinical features of meningitis, Discuss the medical management and nursing management of meningitis.

= **Definition**

Meningitis is defined as an inflammation of the meninges covering the brain and spinal cord.

Bacterial or Pyogenic Meningitis:

It is caused by a wide variety of pyogenic bacterias like Haemophilus influenza, Meningococcus, Pneumococcus, Streptococcus etc. Haemophilus influenza and Meningococcus together account for 70% of all cases of bacterial meningitis. Bacterial meningitis is almost always a complication of bacteremia occurring due to-pneumonia, empyema, osteomyelitis and endocarditis. It is rarely seen but is serious and can be life threatening.

Clinical Features

The typical symptoms of meningitis are rarely seen in children less than two years of age. The onset of symptoms is acute in case of bacterial meningitis but insidious in case of viral meningitis. The clinical presentation of the child with meningitis depends primarily on child's age and etiologic agent. The clinical features in neonates include:

Poor Feeding

Vomiting

Diarrhea

Lethargy

Weak cry

Sleepiness

Presence of full fontanel

The clinical features in infants older than 3 months include:

Fever

- Irritability
- Poor Feeding

Vomiting

- High pitch cry
- Seizures
- Bulging Fontanel/ Nuchal Rigidity

The clinical features in children older than 3 years include:

Fever, chills and malaise because of infection.

Headache, Vomiting and papilledema (rarely seen) because of increased intra cranial pressure.

There are signs of meningeal irritation like:

Nuchal rigidity Positive Brudzinski's sign- With patient in supine position, on passive flexion of neck there is involuntary bending of hip and knees.

Photophobia, diplopia and other visual problems due to cranial nerve irritation.

Delirium, deep coma or stupor due to cerebral edema and increased intracranial pressure.

Management

The treatment of meningitis includes:

1. Specific treatment Treatment is started with antibiotics, on the basis of culture and sensitivity report of CSF .The commonly used antibiotics are: Penicillin with third generation cephalosporins. Vancomycim with third generation Cephalosporin, if penicillin resistance is suspected. Cefotaxine/Ceftriaxone with Aminoglycosides.

Duration of Antibiotic Therapy

- 7-14 days depending upon the type of organism.
- 3 weeks in case of gram negative bacteria.

2. Symptomatic treatment

Seizure management

For controlling seizures, Phenobarbitone 10 mg is given intravenously.

Dilantin can also be given in a dose of 7 mg/kg body weight. Diazepam 2.5 mg may be given to reduce restlessness.

b. Management of increased Intra cranial pressure

Mannitol -0.5 mg/kg body weight as 20% solution is administered. Frusemide 1mg/kg body weight may be given.

C. Fever and headache Aspirin or acetaminophen may be used to manage fever and headache.

3. Supportive Care

IV fluids to maintain fluid-electrolyte balance.

Patients with septic shock require vasoactive drugs like epinephrine and dopamine.

Nursing Management

1. Isolate the child

- When child is admitted with suspected meningitis, the nurse should isolate the child, in order to protect others patients from infection.

Proper isolation techniques and strict hand washing needs to be observed and the parents of the child need to be instructed accordingly.

- Nobody with upper respiratory tract infection should attend the child as he is already infected.

2. Administration of drugs

- Antibiotics and anticonvulsants should be administered as prescribed by the physician. Intravenous antibiotics are given for minimum 7-10 days.

3. Control seizures and protect the child from injury

Since the child is prone to seizures, the child must be protected from injury.

- Monitor the child's level of consciousness.

Side rails of bed should be up and padded to prevent falls.

Never leave the child alone.

4. Maintain fluid intake and nutrition

If the child is unconscious, intravenous fluids are given to meet the nutritional requirements of the body.

If the child's condition permits then nasogastric feeding can be given.

Maintain intake and output record to assess for any fluid retention, impending shock and SIADH (Syndrome of inappropriate anti diuretic hormone). In presence of SIADH, administer only $2/3^{rd}$ of the total fluid requirement.

When oral feeds are started, the diet should be rich in protein, calories and vitamins.

5 . Provide comfort and rest

The child may have photophobia so avoid bright light in patient's room.

The environment of the child's unit should be calm, quiet and thermoneutral to ensure adequate rest and sleep.

Avoid use of pillow as the child is having nuchal rigidity and giving pillow under the head may cause discomfort.

Position the child on side so as to prevent any aspiration (if child is unconscious).

- Care should be taken while moving and lifting the child as this may lead to pain and discomfort.

Head and neck should be supported while lifting the child. Provide passive exercises to the child.

Other comfort measures include frequent mouth care, changing of position to prevent bed sores, use of air or water mattress and keeping the skin clean and dry.

6 . Monitor the child's condition

Vital signs should be monitored frequently. Assess the neurological status and level of consciousness frequently.

Assess the fontanels and measure head circumference daily. Maintain a record of head circumference of the child. An increase in head circumference indicates development of hydrocephalus.

7 . Parental Guidance and support

Inform the parents about the child's disease and his condition. If the child develops deficits, teach them about care of the child at home. Referrals are made as necessary to provide support to the child and family

Q 20. Define hydrocephalus, What are the causes of the hydrocephalus, list the clinical features of hydrocephalus.

= **Definition**

Hydrocephalus is defined as an imbalance between the production and absorption of cerebrospinal fluid It is characterized by abnormal increase in the volume of cerebrospinal fluid within the intracranial cavity resulting in enlargement of the infant's head

.

- **Clinical Features**

The clinical features of hydrocephalus depend on : .

Age of the child

Whether fontanelle have closed or not

Whether cranial sutures have fused

- Type of hydrocephalus

Clinical Features in Infants :

There is accumulation of CSF in ventricles leading to enlargement of the skull .

Sutures become widely separated

Delayed closure of anterior fontanele

Tense bulging fontanele

A hollow or " cracked pot " sound is heard on percussion of skull (Macewen's sign)

Scalp veins are prominent and scalp appears shiny .

The eyes may have a wide bridge between them and visible sclera above the iris (sun setting sign)

Neurologically , the infant may be fussy , restless , irritable , apathetic or have an altered or diminished level of consciousness accompanied by sluggish pupillary response to light , posturing and spasticity of lower limbs .

• In addition , there may be feeding difficulty and high pitch cry due to increased intracranial pressure .

The infant may have physical or mental developmental retardation .

Clinical Features in Older Children

In older children there is no enlargement of head , but there is increase in intracranial pressure resulting in :

Headache on awakening in the morning

Nausea and vomiting

Irritability and high pitch cry

Lethargy

Apathy

Confusion

Impaired judgement and reasoning skills

Affected motor abilities (ataxia , spasticity)

Papilledema , Strabismus or decreased visual acuity secondary to compression of optic nerve

Causes of Hydrocephalus .

Non-communicating or obstructive hydrocephalus may occur due to congenital reasons or it may be acquired.

Congenital causes •

- Stenosis of aqueduct of sylvius
- Meningomyelocele
- Dandy-walker syndrome (obstruction of foramen of luschka or magendie)
- Arnold-chiari malformation (a brain defect resulting in herniation of cerebellum, medulla, pons and fourth ventricle, through an enlarged foramen magnum)

• **Acquired causes**

During the neonatal period and early infancy causes that lead to hydrocephalus are:

- Infections caused by rubella, cytomegalovirus and toxoplasmosis
- Spontaneous intracranial hemorrhage
- Intracranial tumors like medulloblastoma, craniopharyngioma or astrocytoma
- Head injury.

The causes responsible for communicating hydrocephalus are:

- Subarachnoid hemorrhage
- Meningitis
- Toxoplasmosis or Cytomegalovirus infection in which there is obliteration of sub arachnoid space due to inflammatory reaction.
- Diseases of connective tissue like hurler's syndrome and achondroplasia.

Management

Management of hydrocephalus is directed towards :

a . Relief of hydrocephalus or reducing the intracranial pressure

b . Prevention and management of complications

c . Managing problems caused by the pathology

The treatment of hydrocephalus depends on the cause . Medical management includes the use of osmotic diuretic - Acetazolamide and Frusemide to reduce the rate of CSF production . These medicines provide temporary relief but the main management is surgery for removal of any space - occupying lesion and insertion of a shunt .

A shunt is made up of radio - opaque plastic and has a ventricular catheter , a unidirectional pressure valve , pumping chamber and a distal catheter that directs the flow of CSF from the ventricles to other areas of body from where it is absorbed . Thus the shunt helps in removing excessive CSF from the ventricles , thereby reducing the increased intracranial pressure .

Four types of shunts are available :

1. Ventriculoperitoneal shunt
2. Ventriculoatrial shunt (from ventricles to left atrium)
3. Ventriculopleural shunt (from ventricles to the pleural cavity)
4. Ventriculoureteric shunt (from ventricles to the ureter)

The ventriculoperitoneal shunt carries the CSF from ventricles to the peritoneal cavity . It is most has large space to accommodate the coiled catheter tubing . commonly used , as peritoneal cavity provides adequate blood supply to ensure reabsorption of CSF and has a large space to accommmpdate the coiled catheter tubing.

The complications that may arise with shunt include kinking , separation or plugging of shunt tubing . The most serious complication is infection that mostly occurs within two months of surgery . Infection of shunt may lead to ventriculitis and septicemia . Conservative treatment for shunt **infection is administration of antibiotics .**

Nursing Management

Pre – operative

Nursing Care Nursing care in the preoperative period focuses on recognition of signs of increased intracranial pressure , providing supportive care and preventing complications . Nurses must provide the following care :

1. Measure the head circumference of the child daily .
2. ii . Palpate the fontanele for evidence of increased intracranial pressure . The anterior fontanelle is bulging and tense .
3. iii . Due to raised intracranial pressure , the sutures may appear to be widely separated .
4. . Assess the pupillary response and level of consciousness .
5. . Monitor vital signs regularly . Any changes in vital signs should be promptly reported .
6. . As the infant is irritable and restless , provide calm and quiet environment so that the infant may take adequate rest .

7. . Prevent the child from nosocomial infections by using barrier nursing and strict aseptic techniques while providing care .
8. Position the body with neck adequately supported .
9. As the scalp becomes thin , there is an increased chance for breakdown of scalp so , a water pillow or lamb's wool may be used to keep head over it .
10. Change the infant's position frequently .
11. Support the infant's head and neck while handling because the head may too large and neck muscles may be too weak to support the head .
12. The infant is prone to vomiting , so provide small , frequent feeding with intermittent burping .
13. Keep the infant clean and dry .

Post- operative Care

i . Post operatively , place the infant in flat position to prevent rapid CSF drainage and on unoperated side to avoid pressure on the valve of shunt . If CSF is drained too rapidly , there is a risk of subdural hematoma caused by tearing of the vessels secondary to the cerebral cortex pulling away from the duramater . Check vital signs every 15-30 minutes in immediate post - operative period .

11 . Assess the neurological status and level of consciousness frequently .

iii . Assess the head circumference regularly .

IV . V. Monitor the intake and output , as fluids may be restricted during first 24 hours post operatively .

vi . Oral rehydration must be started after the bowel sounds reappear . vii . Check dressings for any drainage .

viii . Meticulous skin care should be provided .

ix . The child must be observed for signs of infection such as fever , increased heart and respiratory rate , poor feeding or vomiting , altered mental status and local symptoms such as redness or CSF leakage at the surgical site .

X. If the fontanele becomes sunken , notify the physician immediately . Also immediately lower the head end of the bed to decrease the outflow of CSF through the shunt . This will help in reducing the risk of subdural hematoma .

xi . Prophylactic antibiotics are administered as prescribed to prevent infections .

xii . Teach parents about care of the child at home , after discharge from hospital . Tell them about

a . Handling the baby while feeding and positioning the child .

b . Recognizing the signs of increased intracranial pressure and malfunctioning or blockage of shunt .

c . Pumping of the shunt in case of increased intracranial pressure .

d . Preventing constipation if the child has Ventriculoperitoneal shunt , as straining during defecation may increase the intracranial pressure .

e . Importance of follow up care .

Q 21. Spina bifida

= Spina bifida is a neural tube defect where there is an incomplete closure of the vertebrae and neural tube .

Definition

Spina bifida is a malformation of spine , in which posterior portion of lamina of vertebra fail to close with or without defective development of spinal cord .

Incidence and Etiology

Spina bifida is the most common developmental defect of central nervous system , occurring in about 1 or 2 per 1000 live births . Spina bifida may occur in any area of spine but most commonly occurs in the lumbosacral area .

The etiological factors associated with spina bifida are : **(Causes)**

Genetic : A child of parents with spina bifida carries 15 times more probability of inheriting the defect .

ii . Maternal Age : The disorder is twice more common in pregnant mothers over 35 years of age or below 20 years of age .

iii . Environmental : Radiations increase the risk of defective neural tube development . Regional differences are also seen . The incidence of spina bifida is more in Great Britain . It is three times more than in USA .

iv . Diet : Folic acid deficiency in the diet of pregnant mother increases the risk of meningomyelocele in the baby .

Classification

Spina bifida is of two types :

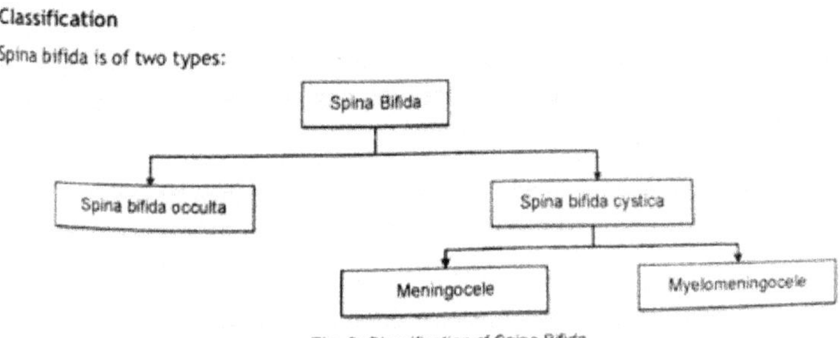

Fig. 8: Classification of Spina Bifida

1. Spina bifida occulta : It is a defect which results from failure of formation of bony arch around the spinal cord , but spinal cord and meninges are normal . It is not visible externally and is asymptomatic This type of defect occurs in 5 % cases of spina bifida .

2. Spina bifida cystica : Spina bifida cystica is a defect in the closure of posterior vertebral arch with protrusion of spinal cord and meninges through the defect .

a . Meningocele : It is a sac - like herniation through the bony malformation , containing meninges and cerebrospinal fluid . The covering of the sac may be thin and translucent or membranous .

b . Myelomenigocele : It is a sac like protrusion of spinal cord , CSF and meninges through spinal cleft . During the embryonic life , the lumbar segment of spinal cord is the last part of neural tube to close , therefore in most of the cases , menigomyelocele are found in lumbar or lumbosacral region .

The defect may occur in lumbosacral region (70 %) , lower lumbar region (47 %) , upper lumbar region (23 %) and sacral region (2.6 %) .

Pathophysiology

Spina bifida occurs because of defect in the orderly closure of vertebral column and formation of spinal cord during 4th to 6th weeks of gestation . During the 3rd week of gestation , a depression forms in the dorsal of the ectoderm in embryo . This depression becomes deeper and its margins close dorsally to create neural tube . The ends of the neural tube close by the end of 4th week of gestation . The walls of neural tube thicken and become spinal cord and brain . The neural canal becomes ventricles and central canal of spinal cord . The vertebral column is formed simultaneously with the neural tube . The exact mechanism by which neural tube defect occurs is not certain .

Two theories are proposed regarding the occurrence of defect :

a . Neural tube fails to close normally or

b . Neural tube ruptures after having once closed

Clinical Features

A. Spina Bifida Occulta

Most of the patients with spina bifida occulta are asymptomatic . The only features seen are : A dimple in the skin or growth of hair over malformed vertebra As the child grows , he may develop foot weakness or disturbances of bladder and bowel sphincter .

Progressive deformity of the foot

Change in micturation pattern

Alteration in gait

Tropic ulcer on the toes and feet .

B. Spina Bifida Cystica

a . Meningocele

• An external cystic defect can be seen at the back . The sac is composed only of meninges and is filled with CSF . The spinal cord and nerves are normal . There is seldom evidence of weakness of legs or lack of sphincter control .

b . Myelomeningocele

Seen in 1 out of every 800 infants , manifestations of myelomeningocele depend on the location and extent of defect . The higher the deformity the more neurological deficits will be present .

- A round , raised , poorly epithelialized , herniated mass is present over the vertebral column , mainly in the lumbosacral region .

Approximately , 90 % of infants with severe spina bifida develop hydrocephalus due to associated Arnold - chiari syndrome .

Loss of motor control and sensation occurs , below the level of lesion .

1. A low thoracic lesion may cause total flaccid paralysis .
2. A Sacral lesion leads to weakness of the lower limbs .

Bowel and bladder may or may not be affected ; there may be fecal and urinary incontinence .

There may be renal impairment due to faulty renal innervation . Urinary tract infections are common complication associated with the defect .

Congenital skeletal anomalies may be present in these children due to denervation of muscles like club foot , developmental dysplasia of hip , kyphosis or scoliosis . These deformities are not only a cosmetic problem , they may also lead to back pain , respiratory distress , recurrent skin breakdown and difficulty in movement .

Developmental delays are commonly seen in speech , mobility etc.

Diagnostic Evaluation

1. Prenatal diagnosis of neural tube defects is possible by using following tests :

a . Ultrasound

b . Fetal MRI

C. Amniocentesis : It may reveal an increase in alpha - fetoprotein , a fetal specific gamma - globulin in the amniotic fluid that indicates presence of meningomyelocele . This test should be done between 14th to 16th week of gestation in all the pregnant females who are at risk .

ii. Diagnosis after birth is made on the following basis :

a . On neonatal examination , a sac may be seen on the back of the baby b . If a lesion is present , its contents can be determined using trans - illumination test (shining light through the sac) . If the sac becomes translucent when light source is held to it , it is a meningocele , if the sac does not become translucent , it is a myelomeningocele .

c . CT Scan and MRI of spinal cord and brain are used to determine bony deformities and spinal cord herniation . They also help in diagnosing presence of other structural defects like hydrocephalus or Arnold - chiari malformation . etc may be done .

d . Laboratory tests like urine test for presence of infection , Renal function test , WBC counts , ESR

e . Other tests include neurological assessment for motor response and sensory reactions , developmental assessment to detect any delay in milestones etc.

Management

The management of spina bifida depends on the nature and extent of defect . Usually no intervention is required for spina bifida occulta . For spina bifida cystica surgery is required - Laminectomy and closure of the defect or removal of the sac is done within 24-48 hours of birth . T - Closure of skin graft is done .

A co - ordinated multidisciplinary team approach is required to maximize the physical and intellectual potential of each affected child . A team of neurologist , neurosurgeon , orthopedic surgeon , urologist , primary care provider , nurse , speech therapist and physiotherapist need to work together for managing the child .

Nursing Management

The main aims of pre and post - operative nursing care are : Prevention of infection

- Preventing injury to the sac
- Prevention of skin breakdown .
- Preventing urinary tract infection Preventing leg and hip deformities Provision of adequate nutrition.

Q 22. Define and write the classification of Epilepsy / Seizures. Clinical manifestation of Status Epilepsy. Nursing management of Epilepsy .

= **Introduction**

Epilepsy is a disorder in which a person has repeated seizures.

Definition

Convulsions are a series of forceful involuntary contraction and relaxation of voluntary muscles due to disturbance of brain function.

Convulsions are abnormal, involuntary, paroxysmal, motor, sensory, autonomic or sensorial changes resulting from abnormal electrical discharges from the brain.

Classification of Seizures

The international classification of epilepsy is currently used to classify seizures. This classification broadly divides seizures into two:

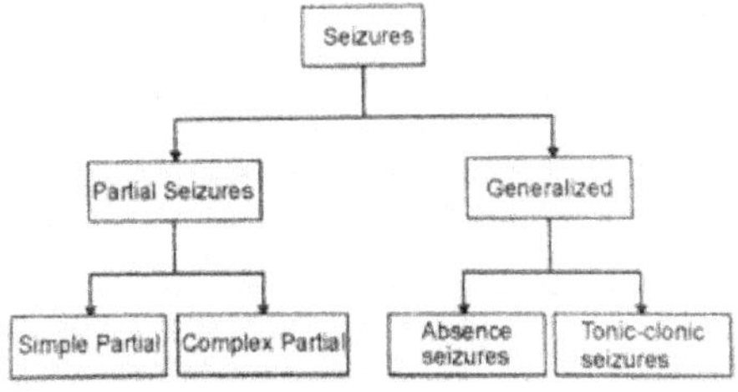

Fig. 11: Classification of Seizures

1. Partial Seizures : Partial seizures begin focally and result from abnormal electrical discharges from a circumscribed small portion of brain.

Partial seizures affect awareness or memory of events before, during and immediately after seizures.

2. Generalized Seizure :

Generalized seizures involve abnormal electrical discharges from both cerebral hemispheres. Motor abnormalities, if any are bilaterally symmetric. Consciousness is always impaired. Absence seizures and tonic-clonic seizures are examples of generalized seizures.

Generalized Seizures

a. Tonic-clonic seizures (Grand mal)

b. Absence seizures:

i. Typical (petit mal)

ii. Atypical

c. Atopic seizures (drop attacks)

d. Myoclonic seizures.

Partial Seizures

a. Simple partial seizures (with elementary symptoms and no impaired consciousness)

i. With motor signs (Jacksonians or focal motor)

ii. With somatosensory or special sensory, i.e. visual or auditory.

iii. With autonomic manifestations (abdominal epilepsy)

b. Complex partial seizures-

Manifested with impaired consciousness and with automatism. It includes psychomotor or temporal lobe seizures.

Status Epilepticus

It is a state of continuing or recurrent seizures that prolonged for more than 30 minutes or occur in a series without regaining consciousness in between attacks. It is a medical emergency as cerebral damage may occur due to prolonged cerebral hypoxia or hypoglycemia. In postictal state, the child may have ataxia, aphasia and mental sluggishness. Mortality rate due to this condition is about 4 percent. The child may have cardiorespiratory arrest or aspiration of vomitus. Residual neurological deficits may develop in 9 percent cases. Todd's paresis or postictal paralysis may result due to metabolic exhaustion of epileptic neurons.

The symptoms include: Clinical Manifestation

Abnormal muscle contraction

Muscle contraction/relaxation

One side of the body is affected

Abnormal head movements

Forced turning of head

Automatism:

- Repetitive purposeless movements
- Starring spells Lip smacking Chewing/swallowing without cause

Abnormal sensations

Numbness, tingling, crawling sensation on the skin.

May occur in only one part of body or may spread.

May occur with or without motor symptoms.

Hallucinations (Auditory or visual)

Abdominal pain or discomfort

Flushed face and dilated pupils

Other symptoms include: Black out spells Changes in vision Changes in mood or emotion and confusion in the post-ictial phase.

Nursing Management

Nurses should be prepared to administer emergency treatment to seizures patients and should instruct family members concerning first aid measures.

Emergency care during seizures

- It includes the following:
- Assist the child to a lying position.
- Take off eye glasses, if the child wears and loosen tight clothes.
- Remove dangerous objects from the viscinity of the child.
- Maintain patent airway and adequate oxygenation must be ensured.
- Administer the prescribed medications on time.

- Do not restrain the child during seizures.
- The side rails of bed should be padded.
- Do not force anything into the child's mouth during seizures.

Care of the child after seizures

- After the seizures are over, the child should be provided complete bed rest.
- Change the clothes and bed sheet, if soiled.
- Suction the airway, if excessive secretions are present.
- Turn the face of the child to one side, to avoid aspiration of secretions.
- Give CPR if breathing is not re-established after the attack.
- Observe the child until fully conscious.
- Treat any injury that may have occurred during convulsions.
- Continuously monitor the vital signs of the child.
- After the child is awake and fully conscious, give oral fluids like fruit juice, lemonade etc.
- Administer intravenous fluids if oral intake is less.
- Maintain intake and output chart. Provide a non-stimulating, calm and quiet environment to the child.
- Parents need to be counseled regarding the disease and its prognosis.
- Parents should be taught how to take care of the child at home.
- The child should not be left alone and should not be allowed to perform activities which involve risk of injury.
- The child who is a known case of epilepsy should wear a medical identification card.

H . DISORDER OF MUSCULOSKELETAL SYSTEM

Q 23. CLUB FOOT

= **Introduction**

Club foot is a congenital anomaly of the foot and lower leg, involving abnormalities of bony architecture and soft tissue. The foot may be divided into the forefoot (toes and metatarsals), midfoot (cuneiforms, navicular, cuboid) and the hind foot (talus and calcaneus).

Although the tibiotalar joint (ankle) provides plantar flexion and dorsiflexion, the subtalar joint (between talus and calcaneus) is oriented obliquely, providing inversion and eversion. Inversion represents a combination of plantar flexion and varus, and eversion involves dorsiflexion and valgus. The talonavicular and calcaneocuboid joints connect the midfoot with the hind foot.

Definition

The term club foot is used to describe a common deformity in which the foot is twisted out of its normal shape or position. Any foot deformity, involving the ankle is known as 'talipes' derived from 'talus' meaning ankle and 'pes' meaning foot.

The clubfoot deformity can be positional or congenital.

Positional club foot is a normal foot that has been held in a deformed position in utero and is found to be flexible on examination.

The congenital club foot involves genetic factors and defects like Edward's syndrome.

Growth arrest at roughly 9 weeks and compartment syndrome of affected limb causes congenital club foot.

Incidence and Etiology

Congenital club foot is seen in approximately 1per 1000 live births.

clinical Features

clinical features of club foot includes

- Adduction of the forefoot or metatarsus adductus.
- Contracture of Achilles tendon leading to equinus position or plantar flexion of the foot.

- The foot is also inverted so the lateral border is directed downwards.
- Development of lower leg is also affected and the calf muscles appear thin and atrophic.

Nursing Management

Nursing Diagnosis are as follows

i. High risk or impaired skin integrity related to application of casts.

ii. Parental anxiety and grieving related to impaired adjustment to anomalous condition.

iii. High risk for body image disturbance related to residual or recurrent deformity.

i Nursing objective: To maintain the skin integrity.

Nursing Interventions:

After surgery, the child has to undergo repeated casting so skin integrity needs to be taken care off.

The nurse should assess the condition of skin under the cast.

A cast that is too tight can put pressure on the neurovascular structures. So the caregivers must be taught how to assess the neurovascular status of the toes.

The skin at cast edges must be frequently assessed and provided care.

ii. Nursing objective: To support the family through anxiety or grieving.

Nursing Interventions:

- The family members should be given an opportunity to verbalize their feelings, concerns and fears.

The nurse must encourage the parents to view the child as a whole and not just the club foot deformity.

The nurse must support the caregivers throughout the treatment.

iii. Nursing objective: To promote healthy body image.

Nursing Interventions:

It is frustrating to have a residual or recurrent deformity. The nurse should provide information to the family about further treatment options.

The nurse must encourage the family for constant follow up till the child reaches skeletal maturity.

The child with residual deformity should be encouraged to participate in age appropriate physical activities.

I . COMMON COMMUNICABLE DISEASES.

Q 24. MEASLES

= Measles is an acute, infectious disease manifested by fever, cough, coryza, lacrimation and koplik'sspots in pre-eruptive phase and maculopapular rash starting on 4th or 5th day of illness.

Epidemiology

Agent:

Measles is caused by RNA virus belonging to paramyxoviridae family.

Reservoirs of infection: Man is the only reservoir of infection.

Transmission of infection: By droplet infection from secretions of nose and throat usually 4 days before and 5 days after appearance of rashes.

Incubation period: 8-12 days Occurs in preschool children In all seasons, more in winter and spring months

- **Risk Factors**

Unvaccinated children

Children with immune deficiency due to HIV

Leukemia

Corticosteroid therapy

Malnutrition

Vitamin A deficiency.

Clinical Features

A. Prodromal Phase/Catarrhal stage (Enanthema)

i. Onset is acute with moderate elevation of

- Temperature
- Hacking cough
- Running nose Sneezing
- Redness of eyes
- Excessive lacrimation

ii. On 2nd on 3rd day of illness 'Koplik's SPOTS' appear on inner side of cheek, opposite to lower molar teeth.

- These may be single or multiple and appear as greyish or bluish white grains of sand, surrounded by reddish aerola.
- Koplik's spots increase in number for 2-3 days.

B. Eruptive Phase/Exanthema

Whitish appearance of rash on 4th day

Fever tends to rise.

The early rash is erythematous and blanches on pressure.

Rashes first appears behind the ears, near hairline on forehead, face and neck and spreads to trunk, extremities, palms and soles within 3 days.

The rash now appears brown and doesn't fade on pressure.

As rashes increase fever rises and pruritis occurs

C. Convalescent stage/Decline :

The rash starts disappearing after 4-5 days in same order which they appeared leaving behind a browny desquamation. Anorexia and malaise are present.

A moderate generalized Lymphadenopathy may be seen.

Types of Measles

1. Modified measles

Observed in partially immune individuals.

The symptoms are milder and duration of illness is short.

2. Atypical Measles • Occurs in previously immunized person after exposure to natural infection. Rashes are associated with hepatospleenomegaly and sensory symptoms.

3. Hemorrhagic measles

It is characterized by:

- High fever
- Convulsions
- Delirium
- Stupor
- Coma Bleeding occurs from mouth, nose and bowel and may result in death.

Nursing Management

i. Bed rest in febrile stage.

ii. Isolation upto 4-5 days after rashes appear. The catarrhal stage is highly infective.

iii. Oral hygiene should be attended every 4 hourly.

iv. Skin hygiene should be attended.

Parents should be encouraged to give bath to the child.

V. Care of eyes is important. Wash eyes with warm water to prevent ulceration and soothen irritation.

vi. Oral fluid intake should be adequately maintained during fever. If there is vomiting give intravenous fluids.

vii. Maintain child's nutrition because after measles, child becomes malnourished, PEM is precipitated and also child becomes prone to TB.

- Protein and calorie intake should be high.
- Milk with sugar, egg, juice etc. should be given to the child.

viii. Fever is controlled by PCM and sponging.

ix. Severe cough is relieved by humidification or saline nebulization.

X. Vitamin A, 2 lakh IU, given orally to the children above 1year of age for two consecutive days reduces the severity, complication rate and mortality due to measles.

xi. Management of complications is essential. For respiratory complications -Antibiotics are given.

- Convulsions - Diazepam/ Phenobarbitone may be given.

Prevention

- Live attenuated measles vaccine offers good protection to susceptible children. It is given at 9-12 months with revaccination at 18 months as part of MMR vaccine.
- Passive immunization in exposed infants with Y globulin intramuscular 0.25 ml/kg for children less than 1year of age.

CHAPTER SIX

Management of Behavioural and social problems in children.

Short answer questions:-

Q 1. Behavior disorders

= Behaviour problems are the viewed as discrepancy between the child's behavior and demands placed on him by his parents , teatures and colleagues.

Types of Behavior Disorders

Behavior disorders can be classified as:

1.Habit disorders

Thumb sucking

Nail biting

Tics

Enuresis

Ecopresis

Stealing

Telling lie

Speech Disorders

a. Stammering/stuttering

b. Phonation and articulation problems

Eating Disorders

Pica

Anorexia Nervosa

Bulimia Nervosa

Sleep Disorders

a. Somnambulism

b. Somniloquy

C. Night mares/Night Terrors

Personality disorders

Juvenile delinquency

Temper tantrums

Shyness

Q 2.Thumb Sucking

= Definition

Thumb sucking is defined as non-nutritive sucking of fingers or thumb.

IT IS HABIT DISORDER

Age of Occurrence

Thumb sucking is common in oral stage (0-1 year) as the babies have a natural urge to suck. This usually decreases after the age of 6 months. Many babies continue to suck their thumb to soothe themselves. Most children stop thumb sucking between 3-6 years of age.

Causes of Thumb Sucking

Parental causes

a. Over protection by parents

b. Neglect by parents

C. Strictness of parents

d. Disharmony between parents

Due to teachers

a. Excessive strictness

b. Excessive punitive attitude of teachers

Due to siblings and friends

a. Excessive competition

b. Separation from close friend or sibling

Other causes

a. Loneliness and boredom

b. Tiredness

C. Frustration and anxiety

d. Separation from parents

Problems caused by Thumb Sucking

Thumb sucking in children younger than 4 is not a problem, but if it continues upto 5 years or above, it indicates presence of an emotional problem.

Prolonged thumb sucking may lead to dental problems like malaligned teeth or sometimes malformation of the upper palate of mouth. The child may also develop speech problems like mispronouncing 'T' and alphabet 'D', lisping and thrusting out the tongue while talking. A child with this type of problem needs to be evaluated by a doctor.

Management

Usually thumb sucking can be managed at home and includes parents setting rules and providing distractions. Many experts recommend ignoring thumb sucking in children as most children stop it on their own. Following measures should be adopted by parents:

Do's

- Divert the child's attention. Engage him in play activities.
- The hands and fingers of the child should be kept busy in some interesting activity like drawing.
- Offer praise and rewards to the child for not sucking thumb.
- Distract the child when he feels bored.
- Put gloves on child's hands or wrap the thumb with a cloth or bandage.
- A non-toxic bitter tasting substance can be applied on child's thumb so that he may not suck it.
- Take help of elder children for explanation to younger siblings.

- Encourage the child to socialize.
- If the child is sucking thumb due to anxiety or distress, address the cause of discomfort. Talk to the child and reassure him.

Don'ts

- Do not scold the child or punish him or forcefully remove thumb from the mouth.
- Do not tie the child's thumb and fingers.
- Do not nag, scold or beat the child.
- Do not leave the child repeatedly cold, wet or hungry.

Q 3. ENURESIS

= **Definition**

Enuresis or bed betting is a disorder of involuntary micturition in children who are beyond the age, when normal bladder control is acquired. Bladder control is normally acquired by the age of 2 ½-3 years. If it is not acquired beyond 4-5 years of age, it is abnormal. When bed wetting occurs repeatedly, it is called as **'Enuresis'**.

Types of Enuresis

Enuresis may be of the following types:

1. Primary enuresis: It refers to the condition in which children have never been successfully trained to control urination. There may be delay in maturation

2. Secondary enuresis: It refers to the condition in which children have been successfully trained, but revert to bed wetting in response to some stress. It may be due to parent child maladjustment.

Another classification is on the basis of time of bed wetting:

1. Nocturnal enuresis: It means bed wetting during night.

2. Diurnal enuresis: It means bed wetting during day time.

3. Mixed enuresis: It includes a combination of both nocturnal and diurnal type.

Causes of Enuresis

Inappropriate toilet training: The age at which toilet training is started has an important impact on child. If toilet training is started very early, it produces stress on the child.

ii. Neurological developmental delay: This is the most common cause of bedwetting. There is delayed development in the ability to stay dry. Bedwetting may be due to delay in nervous system's ability to process feeling of a full bladder.

Genetics: Bedwetting has a strong genetic component. Children whose parents were not wetting bed, have only 15% incidence of bed wetting. When one or both parents were bed wetters, the rates jump to 44% and 77% respectively. Genetic research shows that bed wetting is associated with genes on chromosome13 q and 12q.

EMOTIONAL factors: Emotional and psychological disturbance due to death in family, extreme bullying, severe punishment or scolding, jealousy feeling or sibling rivalry and feeling of being rejected create internal tension in the child which may lead to secondary enuresis.

Emotional sexual abuse,

Organic causes: Enuresis may occur due to anatomical defect of urinary tract and bladder, diabetes insipidus, urinary tract infection etc.

Management

1. For management of bed wetting, it is essential to assess the home conditions of the child, his/her socioeconomic status and family conditions. Explore the child- parent relationship. Child's relationship with playmates, teachers and siblings is alsoevaluated.
2. Reassure the child and parents.
3. Try to build the child's self-confidence.
4. Parents should be explained about the factors related to bed wetting.
5. Parents should be asked not to scold, threat or punish the child. Parents are advised not to nag, criticize or reprimand the child

for bed wetting.

6. The child should not be given any liquids like tea or milk after 5 PM in the evening.
7. The child should be habitually made to pass urine before going to bed.
8. The parents should arouse the child after 2-3 hours of sleep and persuade him to walk unaided, to the toilet, to empty bladder.
9. The child is trained to hold urine for longer time. This may be done by making the child drink large quantity of water during day and persuading him to delay emptying bladder as long as possible.
10. **Bed wetting alarms:** Physicians frequently suggest bed wetting alarms, which produce a loud tone on sensing moisture. This helps the child to wake at sensation of full bladder.
11. **Medications:** In very resistant cases Tricyclic Antidepressants like amitriptyline, imipramine and nortriptyline are given orally, at night for 2 months. Desmopressin, which is a synthetic replacement for antidiuretic hormone (ADH) is also given as it reduces urine production during sleep.

Q 4. Pica

=Definition

Pica is characterized by an appetite for substances largely non-nutritive (such as clay or chalk) and the habit must persist for more than one month, at an age when eating such objects is considered developmentally inappropriate. 'Pica' is eating of non-edible substances such as chalk, clay, coal, mud etc.

It is EATING DISORDERS

Types

The subtypes of pica are characterized by the substance eaten, for example:

Amylophagia: Consumption of starch

Coprophagy: Consumption of Animal feces

Geophagy: Consumption of soil, clay or chalk

Hyalophagia: Consumption of glass

Pagophagia: Pathological consumption of ice

Trichophagia: Consumption of hair or wool

Urophagia: Consumption of urine

This pattern of eating should last for at least 1month to be diagnosed as pica.

Causes of Pica

Pica may occur due to acquired taste or neurological mechanisms like iron deficiency or chemical imbalance. Pica is also linked to mental disability. Stressors such as maternal deprivation, family issues, parental neglect, pregnancy, poverty and a disorganized family structure are strongly linked to pica.

Recent researches suggest that pica is a disorder of specific appetite caused by mineral deficiency, in many cases iron deficiency, which at times is the result of hookworm infestation.

Management

Pica may be managed by combination of psychosocial, environmental, dietary and family guidance approach. For pica that appears to be of psychotic etiology, therapy and medications such as SSRIs have been used successfully. Other treatment techniques are as follows:

1. Presentation of attention, food or toys not contingent on pica being attempted.
2. Discrimination training between edible and non-edible items.
3. Detect nutritional deficiencies and treat them. For e.g. Anemia, Hypocalcemia etc.
4. Make meal times pleasant.
5. Meet the emotional needs of child.
6. Don't leave the child alone.
7. Keep the child busy, as boredom may give him time for eating non-edible substances.

Q 5. TEMPER TANTRUMS

= IT IS A PERSONALITY DISORDERS

Definition

Temper tantrum is a behavior problem, where children assert their independence by violently objecting to discipline through the display of anger at uncontrollable level.

Temper tantrums are seen mainly in toddlers. The toddlers express their anger by lying on the floor, kicking or stamping their feet, screaming loudly and sometimes hurting themselves. Few may become stiff and few may have 'breath holding spells' or banging of head.

Causes of Temper Tantrums

Emotional insecurity

Lack of sleep and fatigue

Imitation of adults

Frustration

Unmet needs

Attention seeking

Management

1. Educate the parents that temper tantrums are child's way of releasing frustration so they should ignore them.

2. Parents should talk to the child to find out the cause of frustration.

3. Provide adequate rest and sleep to the child.

4. Parents should show the child that he is loved even though his behavior is disapproved

6. Parents should not be over protective for the child though they should provide security and support to the child.

5. Parents should be good role model.

Q 6. CHILD GUIDANCE CLINICS

= Child Guidance Clinics were started in 1922, as a part of programme sponsored by a private organization 'Common Wealth Fund's Programme' for the prevention of Juvenile Delinquency.

Concept of Child Guidance Clinics For the all round development of a child the child's physical and physiological functioning and the environment to which he is exposed at home and school, should be taken care off.

All this is possible through interaction with and counseling of the child and his family by a health care team including a pediatrician, neuropsychologist, behavioral therapist, speech therapist and special teachers trained in dealing with handicapped children. This is the basic concept of child guidance clinics.

Definition

Child guidance clinics are specialized clinics that deal with children of normal and abnormal intelligence, exhibiting a range of behaviors and psychological problems which are summed up as maladjustments.

Objectives

The objectives of child guidance clinic are:

1. Providing help for children with behavioral problems like pica, bed-wetting, sleep walking, speech defects etc. It includes:

- Interviewing and interacting with the child and his parents.
- Giving appropriate advice and counseling to both child and his parents.
- Behavior modification therapy, if needed.

2. Providing care and guidance for children with mental retardation including

• Counseling of parents regarding mental subnormality of their children.

Providing medical and physical rehabilitation services.

• Advise regarding placement of the child in appropriate schools or vocational training centers.

Forming peer support groups.

3. Providing care for children with learning difficulties, which include

Early identification of cause and type of learning difficulty in the child. Complete physical (including vision and hearing), developmental and neurophysiological assessment.

Services Provided by Child Guidance Clinics

1. Managing behavioral problems
2. Managing learning difficulties
3. Managing emotional problems
4. Managing adjustment problems
5. Managing developmental problems
6. Managing intellectual deficits
7. Managing socio-legal issues.

CHAPTER SEVEN

Extra

Q 1. Neonatal sepsis

= Sepsis is a serious medical condition caused by the body's response to an infection. In newborns, sepsis can cause swelling throughout the body and possible organ failure.

causes sepsis in newborns

Bacterial infections are the most common cause of sepsis. However, sepsis can also be caused by fungi, parasites or viruses. The infection can be located in any of a number of places throughout the body.

Ways by newborns get sepsis

Newborns can get sepsis in several different ways:

- If the mother has an infection of the amniotic fluid (a condition known as chorioamnionitis)
- Premature birth (premature babies are at a higher risk for sepsis)
- Low birth weight of the infant (risk factor for sepsis)
- If the mother's water breaks early (more than 18 hours before the baby is born)
- If the baby is being treated for another condition while still in the hospital
- If the mother's birth canal is colonized with bacteria.

some symptoms of infections in newborns

Symptoms of infections in newborns include:

- Not feeding well
- Being very sleepy
- Being very irritable
- Rapid breathing or breathing pauses (apnea)
- Vomiting or diarrhea
- Fever (temperature over 100.4 degrees F or over 38.1 degrees C)
- Inability to stay warm -- having a low body temperature despite being clothed and wrapped in blankets
- Pale appearance.

sepsis in newborns diagnosed.

Tests for sepsis in newborns can include:

- Blood tests (blood cell counts, blood cultures)
- Urine tests (urinalysis and culture)
- Skin swabs
- Spinal tap (also known as lumbar puncture) to test for meningitis. A spinal tap is a procedure in which a very small needle is inserted into the space around your child's spine to withdraw spinal fluid to test for infections.

sepsis in newborns treated

Babies who have sepsis are admitted to an intensive care unit. Treatments may include the following:

- Intravenous (IV, directly into a vein) fluids
- IV antibiotics
- Medications for fever (rarely used in newborns)
- Extra oxygen and other forms of respiratory support, if needed

Occasionally, babies may need blood transfusions.

Q 2. JUVENILE DELINQUENCY

Of the various behavior problems that are encountered in children, antisocial behavior is the most taxing and troublesome, affecting not only the family but also various levels of society.

Parents refer to these children as bad boys who need to go to the house of correction. Teachers call them incorrigible and beyond correction. The psychiatrist and psychologist call them 'emotionally disturbed' while judiciary has one term for them - 'Delinquents'.

Definition

Juvenile delinquency is an antisocial behavior, in which a child or adolescent purposefully and repeatedly does illegal activities. The Children Act, 1960 in India defines a delinquent as "a child who has committed an offence such as theft, sexual assault, murder, burglary or inflicting injuries, running away from home etc".

Presentation of Antisocial Problems in Children

The common forms of presentation of Juvenile delinquency are:

i. Constant Disobedience

ii. Lying

ii. Stealing

Fire setting

Destructiveness

Cruelty

Truancy from school

viii. Running away from home ix.

. Sexual problems

Drug and alcohol intake with dependence

Gambling

Other forms of delinquency that are not so commonly seen are assault robbery, rape, homicide, burglary, theft, forgery, fraud, trading stolen goods and property, vandalism, prostitution, bootlegging and smuggling.

Etiology

1. Genetics.

2. Body build
3. Sex
4. Age
5. Intelligence
6. Family background

diagnostic

The diagnostic procedure should be carried out carefully and accordingly the following regime may be recommended:

Interview: It is essential to interview in detail, not only the delinquent but also his parents. The interview should preferably consist of a structured procedure to avoid omitting or failure to elicit essential data.

2. Mental status examination: It is also essential to carefully evaluate the delinquent by means of a systematic Mental Status Examination, so as to obtain information about the present mental state and abnormalities that may prevail.

3. Neurological examinations: It is essential that a neurological examination should be carried out in every delinquent to detect any evidence of abnormality.

4. E.E.G: It is most essential to recommend an EEG of the delinquent, in order to rule out any organic cause for the problem.

5. Psychological test: The personality which is totality of an individual's physical, temperamental, emotional and mental make-up is evaluated in case of delinquents by suitable personality tests, like Rorschach's tests, the M.M.P.I etc.

Prevention of Juvenile delinquency .

Prevention of delinquency is often a very difficult problem and can best be described as under:

i. Primary prevention, which extends to the removal of all factors which directly or indirectly, cause delinquency.

ii. Secondary prevention, which aims at prompt diagnosis and treatment of delinquency.

iii. Tertiary prevention, which aims at rehabilitation of delinquents.

- Prevention of juvenile delinquency may extend to marriage guidance that may help to create a happier family.
- Effective family planning so that all children are wanted, is useful.
- Methods to bring- up stage and a balance of discipline
- and permissiveness should be encouraged in parents. An atmosphere of emotional and financial security should be there at home.
- Proper physical care prevents delinquency.
- Close contact of children with parents, also prevents delinquency. children should be taught at prenatal
- The energy of adolescents should be channelised to prevent delinquency

Management

it is difficult to decide, whether the delinquent should be put away in an institution or treated in the comunity.

The therapy for delinquency should be of two types:

a. Preventive therapy: already discussed above

b. Corrective therapy

c. Drug therapy

Corrective Therapies

Corrective therapies used for juvenile delinquents are:

i. Protective therapy, which not only extends to custodial care, but also to probation or parole.

ii. Punitive therapy, with an idea to serve as a deterrent.

iii. Reformative therapy to bring about certain changes in the personality and behavior of the delinquent.

iv. Rehabilitative therapy, which is very essential to assist the delinquent in his progress and give him a new way of living.

Drug Therapy

The use of drug therapy for delinquents is beneficial only in case of aggressive behavior. **Tranquilizers** in adequate dose need to be given. **Chlorpromazine**, given orally in dose of 25-50 mg, three times a day is the best. Also **Haloparidol** can be given orally in dose of 1.5-10 mg, three times a day. In case of severe uncontrolled aggression, injectable route can be used.

Q 3. Reflexes in child.

=

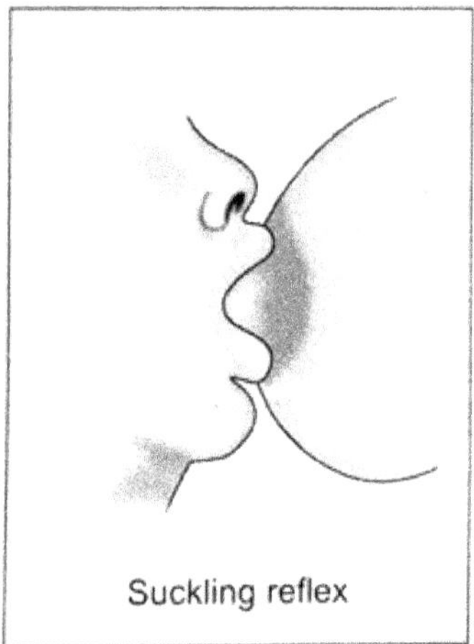

Suckling reflex

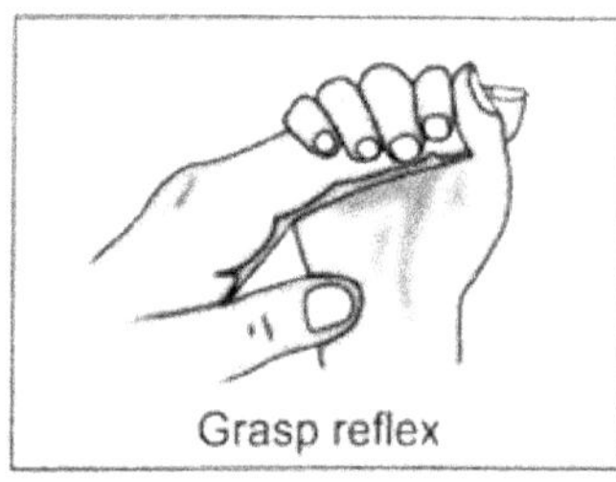

Grasp reflex

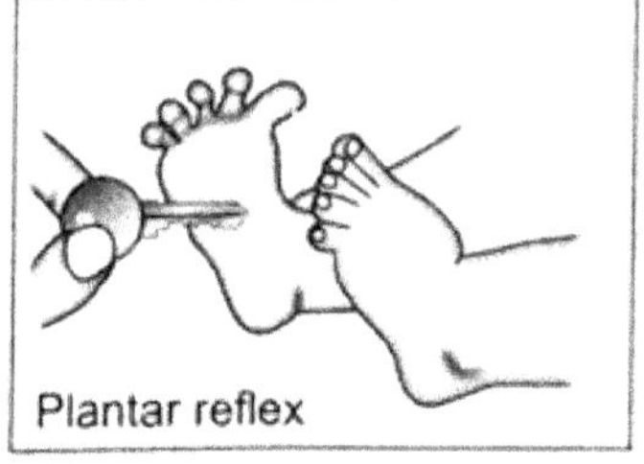

Plantar reflex

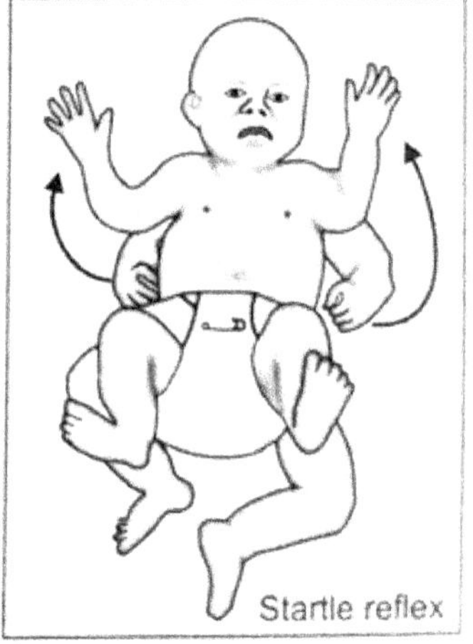

Startle reflex

=

Reflex	Expected Behavioral Response	Age of Appearance	Age of Disappearance
(a) Reflexes of Eye			
1. Blinking	Infant blinks at sudden appearance of bright light or approach of any object towards eye.	Birth	Does not disappear
2. Pupillary Reaction	Pupil constricts when bright light falls on it.	Birth	Does not disappear
3. Doll's Eye	As head is moved to right or left, eyes lag behind and do not immediately adjust to new position.	Birth	3-4 months
(b) Reflexes of Nose			
4. Sneeze	Spontaneous response of nasal passage to any irritant.	Birth	Does not disappear
5. Glabellar	Tapping briskly on bridge of nose (Glabella) causes eyes to close tightly.	Birth	Does not disappear
(c) Reflexes of Mouth			
6. Rooting	The infant turns his head towards any object that touches his cheek and actively seeks the nipple and begins to suck.	Birth	3-4 Months
7. Sucking	Baby begins to suck in response to stimulation of circumoral area.	Birth	Persists during infancy
8. Gag	Stimulation of posterior pharynx by food or suction causes infant to gag.	Birth	Persists throughout life
9. Extrusion	When tongue is touched or depressed, infant responds by forcing it outward.	Birth	4 Months

cont...

10. Cough	Irritation of mucous membrane of larynx causes cough.	Birth	Persists Life Long
(d) Reflexes of Extremities			
11. Grasp	Touching palms of hands or soles of feet near base of digits causes flexion of hands (Palmar grasp) and soles (Plantar grasp).	Birth	Palmar grasp at 3 months and plantar grasp at 8 months
12. Babinski	Stroking outer sole of foot upward from heel across ball of foot causes toes to hyper extend.	Birth	1 Year
(e) Mass Reflexes			
13. Moro's	When loud voice is made or there is sudden change in equilibrium, it causes sudden extension and abduction of extremities and fanning of fingers.	Birth	3-4 Months
14. Perez	When infant is prone on a firm surface, thumb is pressed along spine from sacrum to neck, infant responds by crying, flexing extremities and elevating pelvis and head and Lordosis of spine.	Birth	4-6 Months
15. Tonic Neck	When infant's head is turned to one side, arm and leg extend on that side and opposite arm and leg flex.	2nd month	3-4 Months
16. Galant Reflex	Stroking infant back alongside spine causes hip to move towards stimulated side.	At Birth	4 Weeks
17. Dance or Stepping	If infant is held such that sole of foot touches a hard surface, there is reciprocal flexion and extension of legs.	At Birth	3-4 Weeks
18. Crawl	When placed on abdomen, infant makes crawling movements.	Birth	5 Weeks

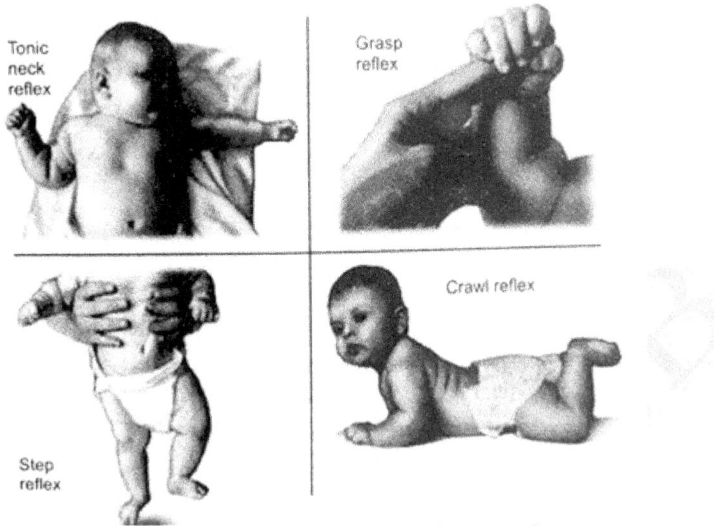

Q 4. Hypothermia

= Definition of Hypothermia

Normal axillary temperature is 36.5-37.5°C. In hypothermia the temperature is below 36.5 degree centigrade. According to severity, hypothermia is classified as

Cold stress-: 36.0°C to 36.4°C

Moderate hypothermia-: 32.0°C to 35.9°C

Severe hypothermia-: <32°C

Prevention of hypothermia

According to the concept of "Warm Chain" baby must be kept warm at the place of birth (home or hospital) and during transportation for special care either from home to hospital or within the hospital. Satisfactory control demands both prevention of heat loss and promotion of heat gain. The "warm chain" is set of ten interlinked procedures carried out at birth and later, which will minimize the likelihood of hypothermia in all newborns.

Warm delivery room (>25°C)

i. Warm resuscitation
ii. Immediate drying
iii. Skin-to-skin contact between baby and the mother
iv. Kangarooing.
v. Breastfeeding
vi. Bathing and weighing postponed
vii. Appropriate clothing and bedding
viii. Mother and baby together
ix. Warm transportation
x. Training/awareness of healthcare providers.

Clinical Features

The manifestations of hypothermia are as follows

i. Peripheral vasoconstriction

- Acrocyanosis
- Cool extremities
- Decreased peripheral perfusion

ii. CNS depression

- Lethargy
- Bradycardia
- Apnea
- Poor feeding

iii. Increased metabolism

- Hypoglycemia
- Hypoxia
- Metabolic acidosis

iv. Increase of pulmonary artery pressure

- Distress
- Tachypnea

v. Chronic signs

- Weight loss
- Poor weight gain

Management

The diagnosis of hypothermia is confirmed by recording actual body temperature.

A hypothermic baby has to be rewarmed as quickly as possible. The method selected will depend on the severity of hypothermia and availability of staff and equipments.

The methods used to manage cold stress include

- Skin-to-skin contact
- a warm room or bed
- a 200 watt bulb
- a radiant heater or an incubator

Infection should be suspected if hypothermia persists despite above measures. Monitor axillary temperature every ½ hour till it reaches 36.5°C, then hourly for next 4 hours, 2 hourly for 12 hours, thereafter 3 hourly as a routine.

ii. Moderate hypothermia (>32 to >36 °C)

Skin-to-skin contact should be in a warm room and warm bed. Warmer/ incubator may be used, if available. Continue rewarming till temperature reaches normal range. Monitor every 15-30 minutes.

iii. In case of severe hypothermia (<32) use air heated incubator (air temp 35-36°C) or manually operated radiant warmer or thermostatically controlled heated mattress set at 37-38°C. Once baby's temperature reaches 34°C the rewarming process should be slowed down. Alternately, room heater or 200 watts bulb or infrared bulb may be used.

Monitor the baby's blood pressure, heart rate, temperature and glucose level. In addition • Measures must be taken to reduce heat loss. 10% Dextrose must be started intravenously at the rate of 60-80 ml/kg/day. • Administer Vitamin K 1mg to term and 0.5 mg to preterm. • Provide oxygen.

Q 6. HYPERBILIRUBINEMIA

= Hyperbilirubinemia or icterus neonatrum is observed during first week of life in approximately 60% of term infants and 80% of preterm infants.

Definition

Jaundice is the visible manifestation of hyperbilirubinemia. Hyperbilirubinemia refers to an excessive accumulation of unconjugated bilirubin in blood resulting in yellowish discoloration of skin and mucous membrane. An indirect bilirubin level of more than 5mg/dl manifests as jaundice.

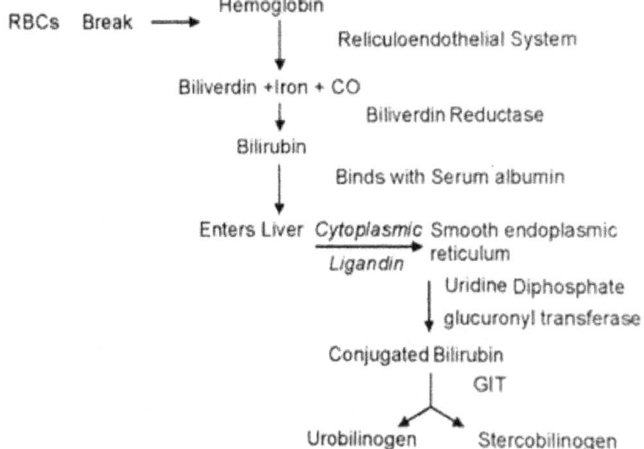

Fig. 1: Billirubin production and Excretion from the body

Bilirubin is formed from the breakdown of RBCs. It is excreted from the body in form of Urobilinogen (through urine) and Stercobilinogen (through stool). Jaundice occurs when the liver can not excrete sufficient bilirubin from the plasma.

Classification

Jaundice is of the following types

1. Physiological Jaundice
2. Pathological Jaundice
3. Breast Milk Jaundice
4. Breast Feeding Jaundice

a. Physiological Jaundice/ Icterus Neonatrum

About 60% of term and 70% of preterm babies develop jaundice within 1st week of life. This is known as

'Physiological Jaundice'. In term babies maximum intensity of jaundice is on 4th day and it subsides by 7th day, whereas in preterm babies maximum intensity is on 5th-6th day and it subsides by 14th day.

Causes of Physiological Jaundice

i. Increased bilirubin load on liver cells

- Increased Erythrocyte volume
- Increased Erythrocyte destruction due to their shorter life span (90 days in children as compared to 120 days in adults)
- Increased Enterohepatic circulation of bilirubin (In newborn's intestine the enzyme B glucuronidase converts conjugated bilirubin into unconjugated form which is reabsorbed by intestinal mucosa and transported to liver. This process is known as enteroheptic circulation)

ii. Defective Hepatic uptake of bilirubin from plasma

- Decreased Cytoplasmic ligandin
- Decreased Serum Albumin Concentration

iii. Defective bilirubin conjugation

- UDPGT activity

iv. Decreased bilirubin excretione& DANS

Feeding the baby stimulates peristalsis and produces rapid passage of meconium, thus reducing the amount of absorption of conjugated bilirubin by stool.

Clinical Features of Jaundice

The clinical Features of Jaundice are

- Yellow discoloration of skin, sclera or nails
- Lethargy
- Refusal to Feed
- Dark urine and stool

Management

1. Pharmacologic management

a. Phenobarbitone: - Phenobarbitone promotes hepatic glucuronyl transferase synthesis which increases bilirubin conjugation. It also promotes synthesis of albumin which increases hepatic uptake of bilirubin for conjugation.

b. Metalloporphyrins: - Metalloporphyrins especially tin-protoporphyrin and tin-mesoporphyrin inhibit heme oxygenase activity thus reducing breakdown of heme to biliverdin.

ii. Exchange Blood Transfusion

Bilirubin can be removed from blood most rapidly by exchange transfusion. It is used when Serum bilirubin is more than 20mg/dl in term infants and more than 15mg/dl in preterms. It is also used when there are serious complications of hyperbilirubinemia. It is rarely used in physiological jaundice.

iii. Phototherapy

Phototherapy is the use of fluorescent light for the conversion of unconjugated bilirubin into conjugated bilirubin.

Author Information

Mr. Rutwik Upendra Bhalshankar .

Mobile No : 9130024431

Email : rutwik61@gmail.com

All Bsc Nursing Books Available On : Amazon , Flipkart, Notionpress.

www.ingramcontent.com/pod-product-compliance
Ingram Content Group UK Ltd.
Pitfield, Milton Keynes, MK11 3LW, UK
UKHW021701190726
13853UKWH00001B/389